153rd LEICESTERSHIRE YEOMANRY
FIELD REGIMENT R.A., T.A.
1939 — 1945

153rd
LEICESTERSHIRE YEOMANRY
FIELD REGIMENT R.A., T.A.
1939—1945

The Naval & Military Press Ltd

Published by

The Naval & Military Press Ltd
Unit 10 Ridgewood Industrial Park,
Uckfield, East Sussex,
TN22 5QE England

Tel: +44 (0) 1825 749494
Fax: +44 (0) 1825 765701

www.naval-military-press.com
www.nmarchive.com

In reprinting in facsimile from the original, any imperfections are inevitably reproduced and the quality may fall short of modern type and cartographic standards.

Contents

		PAGE
Introduction	. . . .	ix
Establishment of Officers on landing in Normandy	.	xi
Officers who joined the Regiment between July 1944 and May 1945	. . . .	xii
Roll of Honour	. . . .	xiii
Personnel Wounded	. . . .	xiv
Personnel Slightly Wounded and Taken Prisoner	. .	xv
Honours and Awards	. . . . . .	xvi

CHAPTER		
I	Formation and Training	1
	Order of Battle	7
II	The Landing and Fighting in Normandy . .	8
III	Pursuit through France and Fighting in Belgium	28
IV	Fighting in Holland and the First Glimpse of Germany	40
V	The Winter	54
VI	From the Reichswald Forest to the Rhine . .	61
VII	East of the Rhine	72
VIII	Events after the Surrender	85
IX	Farewell to Armour	89
X	In Conclusion	99

Illustrations and Maps

ILLUSTRATIONS

	PAGE
129 Battery near Douai . . . . . *facing*	32
Bridge over the River at Nijmegen . . . ,,	33
D.U.K.W.s moving up to the River . . . ,,	33
Railway Bridge at Nijmegen . . . . ,,	48
Leading Tank of 2nd Irish Guards knocked out in attempt to reach Arnhem . . . ,,	49
R.H.Q. Officers at Halmael . . . . ,,	49
Crossing the Rhine . . . . . . ,,	64
Sandbostel Prison Camp . . . . . ,,	64
Wrecked Sherman Firefly . . . . . ,,	65
Part of R.H.Q., near Achim . . . . ,,	80
V.E. Sunday, Cadenberge Forest . . . ,,	80
Ready for G.O.C.'s Inspection . . . . ,,	81

MAPS

Cherbourg and Caen	11
Le Beny Bocage	16
Appendix "B"	19
France and Belgium	30
Albert and L'Escaut Canals	37
Reichswald Forest and the Rhine	64
Western Germany	79

Introduction

IN compiling this history Major Winslow and I have tried to keep it as simple as possible.

The first part has been taken from the Regimental War Diary, and is the story of the Regiment's change from cavalry to artillery, followed by its period of training, up till the landing in France on 29th June 1944.

The second part is the story of the battle, from the day the Regiment landed till the cease-fire, 6th May 1945. This has been taken practically entirely from Lt.-Colonel Jock Atkins' splendid diary and those of 130 and 131 Batteries.

The third, and final, part is very briefly the Regiment's part in the occupational force, the British Army of the Rhine.

BERNARD BRASSEY

Aachen, December 1945.

ESTABLISHMENT OF OFFICERS ON LANDING IN NORMANDY

R.H.Q.
Lt.-Col. J. S. Atkins, T.D.
Major Hon. B. T. Brassey
Capt. S. J. H. Sherrard
Capt. E. C. W. Sowman
Lt. J. H. Paterson
Lt. R. R. Clarke
Capt. G. L. Vokins, M.M.
Capt. A. Ramage, R.A.M.C.
Rev. A. S. Pryor, C.F., R.A., Ch.D.

129 BATTERY
Major Lord Willoughby de Eresby
Capt. D. C. M. Salt
Capt. E. J. Howard
Capt. R. C. Rowland Clark
Lt. J. Gordon
Lt. K. Wharton
Lt. C. D. Tosh
Lt. D. C. Davies
Lt. M. Townsend
Lt. G. Ponsonby
Lt. R. Brisbourne

130 BATTERY
Major R. Hoare
Capt. L. T. Lillingston
Capt. P. Winslow
Capt. A. L. A. Tasker
Lt. S. Hughes
Lt. R. N. Leveson-Gower
Lt. A. C. B. Helps
Lt. D. A. H. Baer
Lt. C. P. Noble
Lt. D. J. Hamilton
Lt. R. E. Tofts

131 BATTERY
Major P. S. Buxton
Capt. Hon. F. Cawley
Capt. M. S. Brown
Capt. S. R. Hedges
Lt. G. A. Huxtable
Lt. J. G. Macalpine
Lt. D. P. Warren
Lt. R. A. J. Ryder
Lt. J. D. Bolton

ATTACHED
Capt. C. E. Akerhielm, R.E.M.E.
Lt. D. Angus, Royal Signals

OFFICERS WHO JOINED THE REGIMENT BETWEEN JULY 1944 AND MAY 1945

R.H.Q.
Capt. P. M. Studd
Capt. J. H. Simpson, R.A.M.C.
Lt. D. M. Colyer, R.A.M.C.
Rev. W. W. March, R.A., Ch.D.

129 BATTERY
Major C. J. Vesey
Lt. B. M. Ross

130 BATTERY
Capt. R. Wright
Capt. J. Green
Lt. A. Baker
Lt. D. Neave
Lt. A. E. Smith

131 BATTERY
Capt. J. C. Reid
Capt. H. Bentley
Capt. H. Yates
Lt. J. McKenna
Lt. G. C. Atkinson
Lt. D. J. Smith
Lt. J. G. Sherer
Lt. F. A. Pearson

ROLL OF HONOUR

Killed in Action:

OFFICERS

Brigadier D. C. W. Sanders, O.B.E., A.F.C., T.D.	June, 1944
Capt. A. Ramage, R.A.M.C.	10 July, 1944
Major P. S. Buxton	18 July, 1944
Rev. A. S. Pryor	3 August, 1944
Lt. J. G. Sherer	10 August, 1944
Capt. L. T. Lillingston	11 August, 1944
Lt. F. A Pearson	8 September, 1944
Capt M. S. Brown	8 September, 1944
Capt. A. L. A. Tasker	20 September, 1944
Lt. D. J. A. Hamilton	22 September, 1944

OTHER RANKS

14324892	Gnr. Short, M. J.	19 July, 1944
14337359	Gnr. Murray, F.	25 July, 1944
822980	Gnr. Ingham, R.	30 July, 1944
554553	L/Sgt. Vines, G. R.	2 August, 1944
14342763	Gnr. Owen, D.	3 August, 1944
952375	Bdr. Trow, W. H. R.	3 August, 1944
325179	Gnr. Norton, A.	3 August, 1944
525149	L/Bdr. Wakeling, L.	3 August, 1944
994275	Sgt. Gullen, J. W.	10 August, 1944
556442	L/Bdr. Wadsworth, R.	10 August, 1944
14345475	Gnr. Corbett, E.	17 September, 1944
982681	Gnr. Nutt, T. A.	22 September, 1944
872329	Gnr. Morgan, H.	26 September, 1944
5734804	Gnr. Scott, E. M.	5 October, 1944
6076696	Gnr. Chatfield, F.	1 May, 1945
978012	Gnr. Randall, T.	1 May, 1945
14276674	Gnr. Wilson, B.	1 May, 1945

OTHER RANKS ATTACHED

Sigm. Blackburn	Royal Signals
Sigm. Spiller	Royal Signals
Sigm. White	Royal Signals

Died:

556513 Gnr. Padgett, J. J. W.	December, 1944

PERSONNEL WOUNDED

OFFICERS

Lt. C. J. Ponsonby	22 July, '44	Capt. Hon. F. Cawley	3 Aug., '44
Capt. S. J. H. Sherrard	25 July, '44	Lt. R. N. Leveson-Gower	3 Aug., '44
Capt. S. R. Hedges	1 Aug., '44	Major Lord Willoughby de Eresby	4 Aug., '44
Lt. T. Ross	1 Aug., '44		
Lt. H. R. Wright	2 Aug., '44	Major Hon. B. T. Brassey	26 Apr., '45

OTHER RANKS

1944

943214 Sgt. Brereton, G.	18 July	4856677 Gnr. Clarke, F.	10 Aug.
1131807 Gnr. Hutchins	19 July	780277 Sgt. Drew, A. L.	10 Aug.
941639 Sgt. Akers, J.	21 July	322959 Gnr. Quinney, R.	11 Aug.
986475 Gnr. Harding, G.	21 July	982679 Gnr. Lathan, T. W.	11 Aug.
2033151 Sgt. Dimond, A.	22 July	348893 Gnr. Coles, A. J.	11 Aug.
325134 Gnr. Padmore, I. R.	22 July	14355574 Gnr. Roberts, G.	8 Sept.
804835 Bdr. Jukes, W. H.	23 July	323839 Gnr. Gibson, B.	8 Sept.
5734625 Gnr. Alden, F. G.	25 July	1711218 Gnr. Brannon, E. E.	8 Sept.
11000260 Gnr. Petty, H. O.	25 July	558006 Gnr. Dunkley, F. T.	22 Sept.
322231 L/Bdr. Fletcher, J.	27 July	327217 Bdr. Toone, P.	22 Sept.
547863 B.S.M. Eady, R. K.	27 July	14320978 Gnr. Ames, W. G.	22 Sept.
11536675 Gnr. Allaker, E.	27 July	558087 L/Sgt. Ellis, T. H.	13 Oct.
557017 Gnr. Coe, F. O.	27 July	818017 Gnr. Gregory, L. A.	14 Oct.
986510 Bdr. Marshall, J.	31 July	557543 Bdr. Wooton, J. A.	14 Oct.
982668 Gnr. Eggleton, M.	3 Aug.	14537661 Gnr. Worral, J. H.	14 Oct.
14374269 Gnr. Morgan, G.	3 Aug.		
981556 L/Bdr. Gay, G.	3 Aug.		**1945**
965630 Bdr. Harris, T. F.	3 Aug.	557457 L/Bdr. Billingham J.	30 Mar.
553709 B.S.M. Freer, F.	3 Aug.	1131931 Sgt. Scott, J. J.	7 Apl.
994660 L/Bdr. Lund, R.	3 Aug.	798159 Bdr. Fellowes, P.	7 Apl.
14367564 Gnr. Thwaites, A.	3 Aug.	943214 Sgt. Brereton, G.	9 Apl.
14337262 Gnr. Duxberry, F.	3 Aug.	14324870 Gnr. Palmer, L. G.	21 Apl.
981565 Gnr. Franks, S.	3 Aug.	891573 Bdr. Akister, N.	24 Apl.
14337437 Gnr. Wild, C.	3 Aug.	7680213 Gnr. Carsley, A.	24 Apl.
553287 Sgt. Corbett, C.	3 Aug.	14576130 Gnr. Choules, C.	24 Apl.
327143 Bdr. Hayes, D.	3 Aug.	14339663 Gnr. Betteridge, F.	1 May
326693 Sgt. Iliffe, J.	3 Aug.	7680213 Gnr. Carsley, A.	1 May
840748 Sgt. Wilson, H.	3 Aug.	986416 Bdr. Core, A. W.	1 May
14377855 Gnr. Wintle, N. K.	10 Aug.	1099695 Gnr. Coyle, E. I. G.	1 May

ATTACHED OTHER RANKS

945761 Pte. Saunders, R. (A.C.C.)   27 July, 1944
210972 Pte. Harris, N. (A.C.C.)   27 July, 1944
Dvr. Booth, J. (R.A.S.C.)   3 Aug, 1944
7643446 Sgt. Gibb, R. (R.E.M.E.)   3 March, 1945

PERSONNEL SLIGHTLY WOUNDED, REMAINED ON DUTY

OTHER RANKS

1944			1944	
14337395 Gnr. Scrimshaw, W.	18 July	553565 B.S.M. George, M.	22 Sept.
5954208 Gnr. Wilbourne, C.	19 July	555658 L/Sgt. Harvey, S. A.	25 Sept.
14324816 Gnr. White, D. W.	20 July	553710 Sgt. Watts, P.	30 Sept.
5886422 Gnr. Coe, A. R.	27 July	106631 Bdr. Colgan, E. W.	27 Dec.
557352 Gnr. Wilson, S. H.	27 July	557449 Gnr. Smith, J. F.	27 Dec.
999079 Gnr. Jacobs, S.	27 July	840750 Sgt. Boston, E. A.	27 Dec.
828063 L/Bdr. May, A. J.	2 Aug.	14298590 Gnr. Humphreys	27 Dec.
1074328 Gnr. Amith, A. G. J.	3 Aug.	14337395 Gnr. Scrimshaw	27 Dec.
5734630 Gnr. Atkins, H. A.	3 Aug.		
14377763 Gnr. Long, K. G.	4 Aug.	1945	
972036 Gnr. Sherring, J.	10 Aug.	1542553 Gnr. Hopkinson, W.	9 Apl.
554552 Bdr. Jackson, G.	11 Aug.	322583 L/Bdr. Hodgkin, H.	9 Apl.
5734872 Gnr. Hampton, W.	22 Sept.	326118 Sgt. Knowles, L. H.	26 Apl.

ATTACHED OTHER RANKS

7653110 Pte. Power, D. J. (A.C.C.)   27 Dec., 1944

PERSONNEL TAKEN PRISONER

OFFICERS

Lt. J. H. G. Macalpine   3 August, 1944

OTHER RANKS

1944		1944	
14353428 Gnr. Withey, R.	3 Aug.	14373753 Gnr. Pratt, H.	3 Aug.
891563 Bdr. Denby, H.	3 Aug.	961747 Gnr. Dolman, J.	3 Aug.
941644 L/Sgt. Parkinson, L.	3 Aug.	1099739 Bdr. Treadaway, V.	3 Aug.
5734904 Gnr. Noyes, F. A.	3 Aug.		

HONOURS AND AWARDS

D.S.O.
Lt.-Colonel J. S. Atkins, T.D.

M.C.
Major R. Hoare
Major C. T. Vesey
Capt. E. J. Howard
Capt. M. M. Townsend
Lt.-Colonel Hon. B. T. Brassey

M.B.E.
Capt. E. C. W. Sowman

M.M.
327115 L/Sgt. Ashwell, N. H.

B.E.M.
553710 Sgt. Watts, P.

Mentioned in Despatches
Lt.-Colonel J. S. Atkins, D.S.O., T.D.
Major Lord Willoughby de Eresby
Major R. Hoare
Capt. P. D. Winslow
Rev. A. S. Pryor, C.F., R.A., Ch.D.
Lt. J. D. Angus, R. Sigs.
Lt. R. A. Ryder
818017 Gnr. Gregory, L. A.
976985 Gnr. Leeman, P.
556331 B.S.M. Marriott, B. J.
553830 B.S.M. Best, C. T.
325184 Sgt. Dighton, V. W.
554650 Sgt. Harrison, A. H.
986482 Bdr. Hefford, C. G.
5734891 L/Bdr. Watts, D. C. F.

Croix-de-Guerre with Gilt Star
Capt. E. J. Howard

Croix-de-Guerre with Bronze Star
828063 Bdr. May, A. J.
2321946 Sgt. Spreadbury, A.E.P., Royal Sigs.

Belgian Croix-de-Guerre with Palm
4868147 Gnr. Reid, P.

CHAPTER ONE

Formation and Training

ON 1st September 1939 a telegram was received from the 5th Cavalry Brigade saying *"Embody."*
On 2nd September this order was carried out, with the Headquarters Squadron ("B") on Oadby racecourse, and the three squadrons remaining in their areas, which were, Oakham ("A" Squadron), Shepshed ("C" Squadron), and Market Harborough ("D" Squadron).
At ten minutes to two on the afternoon of 3rd September a further telegram was received from the 5th Cavalry Brigade saying: "War has broken out."
The Regiment moved on the 22nd of the month to its concentration area at Rufford Abbey, and was transferred to the 6th Cavalry Brigade.
Three days later the first eighty horses arrived; by the end of October the strength of the horses had risen to 513. The time was taken up with squadron and troop training, as well as teaching a number of the younger recruits the finer arts of horsemanship.
During the month of November various rumours reached the Regiment that certain regiments would become dismounted, but were not taken very seriously. However, early in December, a letter was received from the War Office, dated 25th November 1939, inviting the Regiment to change from cavalry to artillery. The Commanding-Officer attended a conference at the War Office and returned with the news that the Army Council had decided that the un-brigaded yeomanry regiments should change their arm to artillery. A choice of guns was allowed, medium, field or anti-tank; the officers were unanimous in their choice of field.

During the months of December and January little training was carried out, owing to hard frost and deep snow. The main object in life was to keep the horses, which the Regiment was to lose so soon, as fit as possible. Training also started in the Regiment's new arm at this time, under Major Friedberger, R.A., so well known in the show jumping world. Towards the end of February the Regiment lost 350 horses to the Royals and Greys in Palestine, the remainder leaving during the course of the next two months.

During March and April training continued as best as possible, but it was not possible to do a great deal owing to the lack of equipment.

In May the first guns arrived, two very ancient looking 4.5 howitzers, on enormous wooden wheels; according to their history sheets they had been passed for drill purposes only in 1924. At last it was possible to start on proper gun drill. By now everybody in the Regiment was very keen on their new weapon and determined to make a real success of it.

At the beginning of June Major Brassey took a composite battery of one troop from 153 and one troop from 154 to the 22nd Armoured Brigade, near Lincoln, for training. The troop from 153 consisting of four 4.5 howitzers and that of 154 of four 18-pounders.

The remainder of the Regiment during this period carried out training as a mobile infantry striking force in its Home Defence role, at the same time carrying on with its artillery training, despite the almost complete lack of equipment. It was a trying time for all concerned, as the Regiment, owing to security requirements, had been confined to barracks since the beginning of May.

June 10th was a great day, as for the first time since becoming gunners the Regiment were to fire their guns. The 4.5 howitzer troop went to Gibraltar Point, 4 miles from Skegness, and fired sixteen rounds, on to the sandbanks. The following day the 18-pounder troop did the same.

Shortly after this, the 18-pounder troop from 154 left the battery and went under command of 1st Division. The battery was then joined by another 4.5 howitzer troop, and moved into gun positions near Holbeach, and also came under command of 1st Division.

On the 1st July this battery moved to the Grimsby area into gun pits, and were in support of the 2nd Bn. Coldstream. Only a week later it received orders to move to an area between Skegness and Boston and join the remainder of the Regiment, which had at last got its guns. Leaving the guns in their pits for 154 to take over, the battery in turn took over the latter's 18-pounders, and on 10th July the Regiment was together once more. "A" Battery, with its 4.5 howitzers, was at Wainfleet, with Major Lord Willoughby in command, and "B" Battery, with 18-pounders, at Old Leake, with Major Brassey in command.

The Regiment was now in its battle positions, and had a large piece of the coastline, between Boston and Skegness, to cover, in the event of invasion on that part of the coast. The guns were in gun pits, and many and varied were the disguises, in an attempt to camouflage the positions, varying from haystacks to hen-houses. At the beginning of August "B" Battery had its 18-pounders taken away and replaced by 75-mms.

For the next two-and-a-half months training continued on normal lines, each battery having its monthly allotment of practice ammunition, which was fired from its gun pits at selected targets over the sea wall. The local inhabitants soon became accustomed to this, and did not even deign to look up as the shells whistled over their heads while they were working in the fields. During this period the G.O.C. 1st Division, also the G.O.C. in C Northern Command visited the Regiment.

On the 19th October the Regiment returned to its own county for the winter and for more intensive training, regimental headquarters being at Pickwell, "A" Battery at Barleythorpe, "B" Battery at Somerby.

During November the Regiment had to form a third battery, which was commanded by Captain Collins and was billeted in Burrough-on-the-Hill, "A" and "B" batteries now becoming "P" and "Q", and the new battery "R".

Also during this month a Signal Section, from the Royal Corps of Signals was posted to the Regiment, as also was a L.A.D. from R.E.M.E., finally completing the personnel.

Training continued for the next three months, with exercises set by the C.C.R.A., Brigadier J. Barrie, who had his headquarters in Oakham; also a visit to Sennybridge in Wales, for a week's practice camp.

At the beginning of March the Regiment moved to the area round Louth, and at the end of the month went under command of the Lincolnshire Division.

For the next six months, up till the end of September, the Regiment remained with the Lincolnshire Division. The training mainly consisting of the close support by field regiment to an infantry brigade. Two demonstrations were given by "Q" Battery, one at Redesdale, on the quick support of a battery, with the infantry, using a No. 18 wireless set, and a second one at Larkhill, to the C-in-Cs—a method which was to prove its worth later in battle.

About the middle of August it became known that the Regiment had been selected to become gunners to the newly-formed Guards Armoured Division, and on 22nd August Major-General Sir Oliver Leese, the Divisional Commander, came down to inspect the Regiment.

On 9th October 1941 the Regiment ceased to be 1st Corps Troops, and set out to join the Guards Armoured Division in Somerset, staying the first night at Lutterworth.

The Honorary Colonel, Col. Abbot Robinson, T.D., accompanied by the Lord-Lieutenant of Leicestershire, took the salute on the by-pass north of Leicester.

The following day the Regiment arrived in its new billets at Frome; its home for the next sixteen months. H.M. Queen Mary visited the Regiment on 21st October. These were sixteen months of intensive training in the role of supporting artillery to an armoured division. During this time were many demonstrations, including one with live ammunition, before H.M. The King.

During the month of October 1942 the Regiment was ordered to find a complete battery, to help form the 192 Field Regiment. This was a great blow, particularly as the replacements were all infantry soldiers, with little training and no knowledge of gunnery.

On 28th February 1943 the army exercise "Spartan" commenced; at the conclusion of this, a fortnight later, the Division moved direct to its new area in Norfolk, the Regiment being in and around Fakenham, where it stayed until July.

In April the King visited the Division, accompanied by H.M. The Queen and the two Princesses, and a demonstration of a field regiment coming into action, followed by a march past was given in Raynham Park.

On 24th April Lt.-Colonel D. C. W. Sanders, O.B.E., A.F.C., T.D., who had commanded the Regiment with so much distinction from the beginning of the war, and whose unbounded energy and drive had turned the Regiment from cavalry into a field regiment second to none, left to take up his new appointment of C.R.A. to the Marine Division.

Major J. S. Atkins assumed command, and was destined to continue as commanding officer until the finish of hostilities.

At the beginning of July the Division moved to Yorkshire to complete its training as an armoured division, a vast area of the Yorkshire Wolds having been taken over by the War Department, to enable tanks to go across country, where and when they wished. The Regiment went into a very comfortable Nissen-hutted camp at Nawton, between York and Scarborough.

In November warning was received that the Regiment was to be converted to a S.P. regiment, with 25-pounders on a Sherman chassis. This was to entail a great deal of further intensive training, to get everybody up to the same high standard with their new weapon.

The first twelve guns and thirteen O.P. tanks arrived in the middle of December. The next four months training continued, and everybody quickly got used to the new guns and tanks. When on 6th April all leave was cancelled, and the following day censorship was imposed, there was little doubt in anybody's mind that the great moment for which we had been training so hard was not far off.

During the first week of May, the Division moved to its

concentration area on the South Coast, the Regiment being in Eastbourne.

The main occupations for the next month were to waterproof all the vehicles, for the expected wade on the far side of the Channel, and the keeping of all ranks fit.

On 18th June the Regiment left by road for Camp C1, in the marshalling area, just outside Southampton; here to remain for ten days, owing to the fact that enough tanks had arrived in Normandy and the great need at that moment was for more infantry.

On the night of the 27th/28th orders were received to move to the embarkation area in the docks.

It was while embarking on the 28th that the sad news was received that Brigadier Sanders had been killed. A loss that was felt equally by all ranks.

After a good trip on American tank landing craft, the Regiment landed in Normandy on 29th June 1944.

ORDER OF BATTLE

Showing the Regiment sub-divided into Groups.

5th GUARDS ARMOURED BRIGADE

IRISH GROUP	GRENADIER GROUP
2nd (Armoured) Bn. Irish Guards	1st (Motor) Bn. Grenadier Guards
3rd Bn. Irish Guards	2nd (Armoured) Bn. Grenadier Guards
129 Battery	130 Battery
Detachments from A/Tank, R.E.s Field Ambulance, etc., etc.	Detachments from A/Tank, R.E.s, Field Ambulance, etc., etc.

R.H.Q.
131 Battery
"A" Troop 94th L.A.A. Regt., R.A.
Signals Section
L.A.D.
Q.M. and "A" Echelon, etc.

With the Irish Group leading with 129 Battery, the other two batteries followed on immediately behind, ready to link up and deploy with 129 Battery should the extra support be necessary, and *vice-versa* with the Grenadier Group in the lead.

On a few occasions the Coldstream Battalions were included in 5th Guards Armoured Brigade, and the group was made up as follows:

1st (Armoured) Bn. Coldstream Guards
5th Bn. Coldstream Guards
131 Battery
Detachments from A/Tank, R.E.s, Field Ambulance, etc., etc.

CHAPTER TWO

The Landing and Fighting in Normandy

I. FIRST BATTLES

After more than four-and-a-half years of preparation ranging from Leicestershire, the coast of Lincolnshire, Somerset, Norfolk and Yorkshire, the Leicestershire Yeomanry at long last crossed the Channel on 28th/29th June 1944, landing at Asnelles sur Mer near Arromanches at 2300 hours, 29th June.

From its winter quarters at Nawton the Regiment moved to Scarborough, which was much enjoyed by everyone after the Nissen huts of Nawton, although the officers who still had a horse or a dog missed them, but it was now time to say good-bye to these friends, who had helped many of them through the long days.

The Colonel, Jock Atkins, had managed to keep a horse and a dog himself all the way through, and Bernard Brassey, James Willoughby, Peter Buxton, Bob Hoare, Luke Lillingston had all found a horse, dog or gun invaluable.

From Scarborough the Regiment moved to a concentration area at Eastbourne on 3rd May, the tracks all going by rail.

On 18th June the final move to the marshalling area at Southampton took place. By the route it had to take, the Regiment covered more than 100 miles over blistering roads and in scorching wind, which did very little good to all the water-proofing efforts, and the driving of heavy tracks tried the drivers to the limit, but in 48 hours the Regiment looked as fresh as paint again.

Owing to the way that the battle was going in the bridgehead, and the fact that General Montgomery wanted more infantry rather than armour, the Regiment stayed at

Southampton for ten days, and, of course, the rough weather that sprang up soon after D-Day, and the difficulties experienced by the Navy in landing on the beaches also slowed things up somewhat. The census of opinion from the men was that they had never been fed better, and were being fattened up for the fray!

Maintenance, route marches and swimming to keep fit were the order of the day. There was a company of dogs for mine detecting in the camp at this stage, and very interesting it was to watch them work.

The call to embark came at an unpleasantly early hour, but it all went without a hitch. Just as the Regiment was about to embark, on a dull, drizzling morning, the news came of the death of Brigadier Dennis Sanders, a great friend and a splendid Commanding Officer of the Regiment. It was a great blow to all who had known him, and only mollified by the knowledge that his primary role in the invasion had already been achieved with the Royal Marines. Each battery had a L.S.T. practically to itself —and one for R.H.Q. also. The crossing was good, and the sight of the hundreds of craft, from battleships to small M.T.B.s, the balloon barrage and the prefabricated docks, were sights that will never be forgotten. The boats in which the Regiment came over were American, and every one enjoyed the novelty of American food.

The Regiment assembled in its concentration area by 0800 hours, 30th June at St. Martin des Entrees, two kilometres from Bayeux. R.H.Q. were in a pleasant orchard and the three batteries in adjacent fields. The inhabitants seemed pleased to see us, and it was a good sight to see our Padre Pryor chatting to a host of small children, who sat round eating sticky bon-bons, of which there was a surfeit in the early days.

At this time the situation in Normandy was as follows— since D-Day continuous penetration had been going on, and the line ran from Caumont-Hottot-Vendes-Grainville-Carpiquet-Cambes-north of Troarn-mouth of River Orne. The battle for Cherbourg was just finishing.

General Montgomery came to talk to the C.O.s in the Division, and he told us his plan was to contain the main German forces on the British 2nd Army front whilst striking down the west side of the battle zone with the American Army.

On 5th July the Regiment received orders to move east to help support our old friends, the 1st Corps, in which it had once served. The Colonel with the second-in-command, Bernard Brassey, and the Battery captains met at the village of Plumetot, and shortly after the Regiment moved into position.

The operation was known as operation "Charnwood," and was a plan involving 3rd Division, 59th Division and 3rd Canadian Division in order to capture Caen. Thirty artillery regiments of all kinds took part, also H.M.S. *Belfast* and *Rodney*.

The enemy at the time were holding Beauregard-Lebisey-Epron and Carpiquet Aerodrome.

On the night of the 7th/8th July the Regiment fired its first rounds in anger, and it was with a feeling of satisfaction, sitting in the command post with Bernard Brassey and other officers of R.H.Q. that the Colonel gave the order *"fire"* and heard all guns thunder out their defiance.

H-Hour was 0420, 8th July, and the attack was planned which involved an advance of all three Divisions, and the Regiment's fire-plan was to lay a barrage on the western half at Lebisey. The positions to the north of Caen had already been softened by a tremendous raid the previous evening by 500 Lancasters. At its position at Plumetot the Regiment had a front-row view of the operation. The Lancasters came over in two waves, and, completely undeterred by fairly heavy flak, proceeded to batter the targets. A large black pall of smoke soon drifted over the gun positions.

The first phase of the attack was completed successfully by 0800 hours.

Later, the Regiment was ordered to lay down a concentration on St. Contest for an hour. This was done, and 3rd Division quickly got through and into ring-contour 60 overlooking Caen itself.

On 59th Division front, however, things went less well, and pockets of the enemy held out at Epron.

At 1130 hours 8th July, the Regiment received orders to support 33rd Independent Armoured Brigade, which was

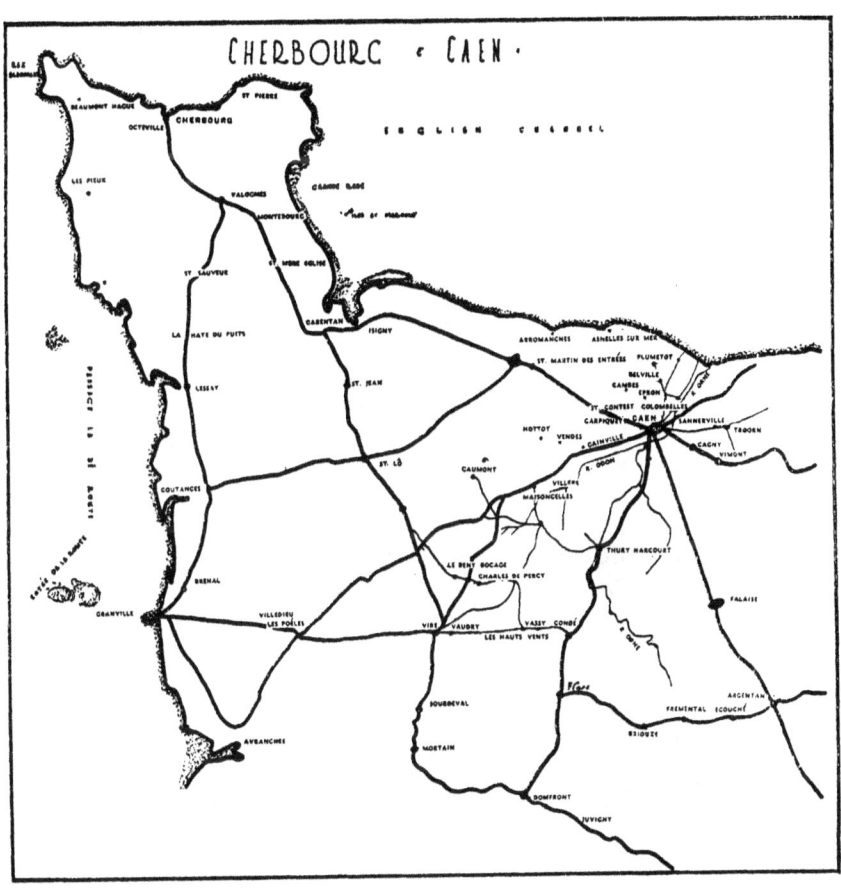

ordered forward. O.P.s went out, and the Brigade pushed down to join the Infantry Brigade H.Q., reaching the remains of Lebisey, where the Colonel stayed the night with Brigadier Scott. Not a very pleasant spot—certainly the barrage seemed to have been effective, as the whole area was shattered, with over 200 dead Germans.

From the ring contour 60, Peter Buxton conducted the first observed shoot. By 1000 hours 9th July, the enemy north of Caen had been dealt with, and infantry from 1st Division were in the town itself. It was practically impassable, and 33rd Armoured Brigade together with the O.P.s were withdrawn.

On the evening of 9th July warning orders to move back to our own division were received. Before it left, the Regiment received its first casualty. The gun area had for some time received unwelcome attention from two enemy guns thought to be 170-mm. east of the Orne. These opened up about 1930 hours, and the first salvo, aimed probably at Plumetot Wood, fell short owing to cold barrels, straddled the R.H.Q. position, and the Doctor, Sandy Ramage was fatally wounded. This was a very great loss, as he was most popular and knew everyone so well.

On the 10th July the Regiment returned to St. Martin to the original fields and orchards, where it remained until the main offensive east of the Orne.

Meanwhile 32nd Brigade had been having some hard fighting round Cheux, with 55th Field Regiment R.A. in support—as yet the armour had not been in battle.

The following extracts from letter received on its first action bear evidence of the good work of the Regiment.

From General Whistler, D.S.O.—"Our battle for Lebisey Wood in operation 'Charnwood' was made comparatively easy for 185 Brigade by the artillery support. I would like your people to know that we appreciated the support of your guns and hope that we shall be able to help you one of these days and give you, too, an easy passage."

From Brigadier Manners Smith, C.C.R.A. 1st Corps—"I write a line to thank you very much for the support that the Guards Armd. Div. Artillery (Leicestershire Yeomanry) contributed to 'Charnwood,' and am glad to hear that the O.P.s of the Leics. Yeo. enjoyed themselves with 33 Armd. Bde. It was a very real pleasure to me to have your party, for which I still have a great sentimental attachment, included in 1 Corps Arty. resources for the operation, and I am grateful to fate for the coincidence that 153 Leicestershire Yeomanry should have made their active service debut under my *aegis*. I should like to think that it is not too much to hope that 1st Corps may find G.A.D. working with it again on some future occasion.

"Many thanks again for your help and support, and best of fortune in whatever lies ahead of you."

Yours ever,

Manners."

Thus, at the end of its first battle it had good reason for satisfaction.

After four days at St. Martin, the Regiment received its orders for the new big offensives, in which the Division's armour would be used for the first time, and on the 16th July the Regiment moved out at night in a long and extremely trying night march to a gun position east of the River Orne, where the 6th Airborne had landed on D-Day. It passed by the spot where Denis Sanders had been killed, and it is nice to record that the Padre and the Q.M. were able to see his grave and put some flowers there.

The O.P.s joined their Armoured Battalions, and moved on the night of 17th/18th July.

The plan was for a break-out by Canadians right, 11th Armoured Division, Guards Armoured Division and 7th Armoured Division centre, and 3rd Division left, and for the factories around Colombelles which had caused so much trouble to be cleared up once and for all.

The attack was preceded at 0530 hours, 18th July, by one of the heaviest aerial bombardments of the war, in the area factories—Cagney, Touffreville, which was very impressive as the Regiment waited in the early hours.

At 0745 hours our artillery barrage began, covering the advance of 11th Armoured Division for about 5,000 yards towards Cagney. 3rd Division on the left cleared Touffreville and later Sannerville.

On the armour's front opposition, initially disorganised by the bombing, got stiffer as the Division pushed south past Demouville, and casualties to the tanks were fairly high. Several Pz. KW.IV's were knocked out.

Alas! Peter Buxton, commanding 131 Battery, was killed in this action. He was acting as O.P. to 1st Bn. Coldstream, and was very unlucky to get a direct hit by an enemy shell just as he was getting out of his tank to go and talk to Colonel Rid Myddleton, commanding the Armoured Battalion. He was a great loss to the Regiment and to all who had known him so long, and known the work he had done.

It was found impossible to push further than Cagney. Meanwhile the Regiment was moving up the "Holly" route with Battalion Groups, and came into action in the evening in the area of the railway Sannerville and Demouville, where it was fairly heavily shelled during the next two days. After this juncture it assisted the 32nd Brigade into Frenoville.

The front line then became static, and on Sunday, 23rd July, the Regiment was ordered to pull back to the factory area at Colombelles to refit. The rest of the Division had already been pulled back, so that when the Regiment arrived back at Colombelles about 1400 hours 24th July, it was greeted with the news that operation "Spring" was to start at 0300 hours the following morning. This meant no time for maintenance, which was very essential as the rain during the days by the railway had been torrential.

The plan was for a thrust in the centre of the tank country due south from Bourguebus, but only phase I of the plan succeeded.

On 26th July the Regiment pulled out into the column at 0700 hours. During the night there had been a considerable amount of bombing, and the Adjutant, Tim Sherrard, was wounded in the legs, in spite of being in a dug-in command post. Tony Tasker came in from commanding "D" Troop to breech the gap.

At 0730 hours orders were received to halt, and for the rest of the day no progress was made and the Regiment returned in the evening to its position near the factory at

Colombelles, where it spent two or three unpleasant days on an open hill, being shelled now and then. Several N.C.O.s and gunners were wounded from 130 Battery, and the "Harboro" boys had ill luck to have B.S.M. Eady and Bdr. F. Fletcher wounded—fortunately not badly.

On 30th July the Regiment pulled out at first light and went back once again to its orchard and fields at St. Martin near Bayeux. The route was through Caen, and there was seen for the first time the full result of a mass R.A.F. raid, a sight which was to become common later on in Germany. The dust still hung in the air, and the sight of the bull-dozers hard at work clearing the rubble to allow for single-line traffic in what was once a main street, is something that will never be forgotten, and yet the few people that were about all had a smile and a handwave for the Regiment, showing their wonderful courage and spirit.

At St. Martin the local inhabitants seemed even more pleased than ever to see the Regiment again. However, this stay was very brief, and we pulled out once again at 0400 hours, 31st July.

2nd Army had attacked the day before at Caumont, and 8th Corps was now to resume its original conformation of Guards Armoured Division, 11th Armoured Division and 15th (S) Division.

The Division now formed itself into battle groups owing to the most unsuitable country in which to operate armour.

On 31st July Bernard Brassey and his "recces" went forward once again to find a position for the Regiment, and it went into action just south of Septs Vents. The Division objective was Vassy.

By nightfall 31st July, 5th Brigade H.Q. was established at St. Martins des Besaces after a difficult day's fighting. This was a most unpleasant spot for Brigade H.Q., which got heavily shelled, being at a very foolish place (*i.e.*, near a village and cross-roads). Unfortunately Sidney Hedges who was doing C.O.'s rep., and was with the Colonel at the time, got one very near, and was wounded in the back.

During the next two days the advance on the Divisional front continued slowly, and fighting at all times was

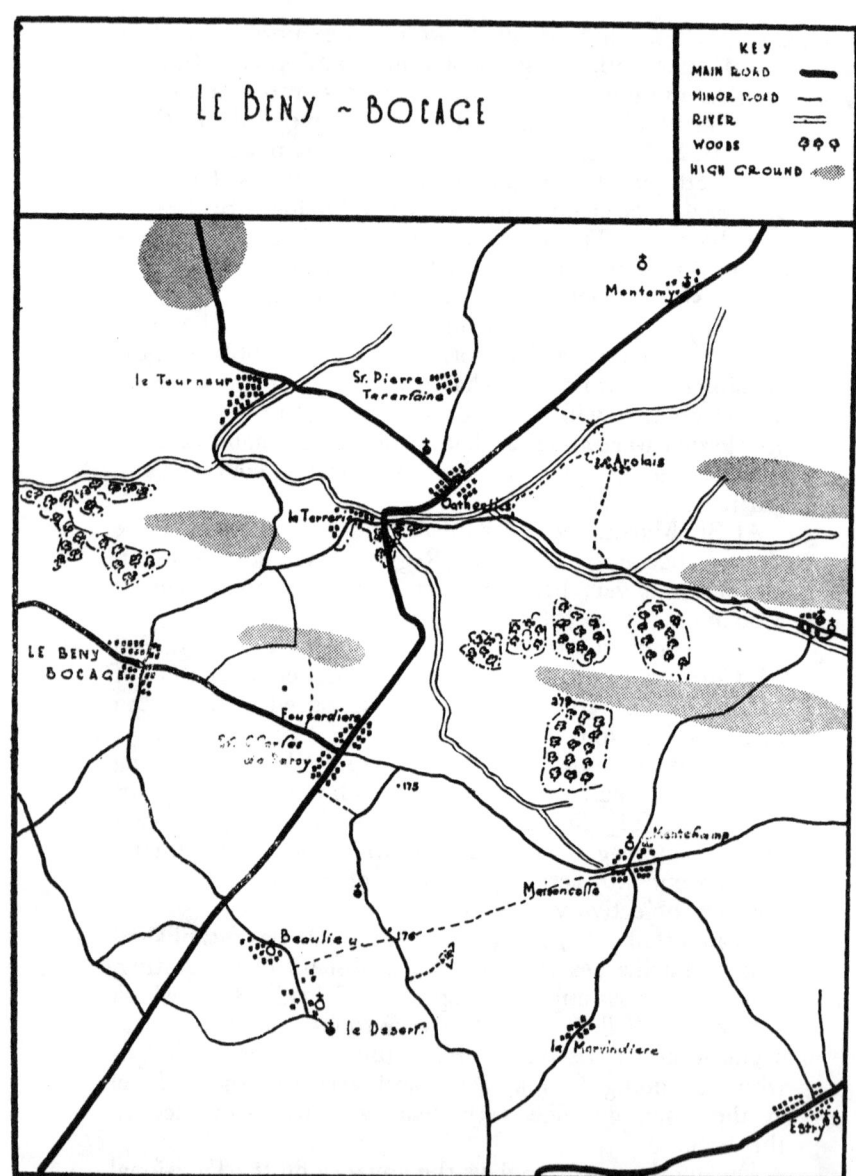

extremely heavy, and not made easier owing to the enormous difficulties of the close country, bad roads and banks.

On the afternoon of 2nd August the Grenadier Group was having a particularly bad time in the area of Catheolles, with one squadron up the road to Montamy. The latter, commanded by James Bowes-Lyon, kept seeing the flash of enemy mortars, and called urgently to Bob Hoare for an O.P. He sent him Roy Wright, who had recently taken over "D" Troop from Tony Tasker. Unfortunately he never got there, as his tank received a direct hit from a shell on the co-drivers hatch which killed Sgt. Vines, who had served the Yeomanry so very well and truly for many years. It also wounded Roy Wright quite badly, and Gnr. Eggleton was shot through the leg by a sniper as he was getting out. Bdr. May and Bdr. Ashwell did great work in getting the wounded back, but they left the tank behind.

During that night, and without saying a word to anybody, Bdr. May went back by himself to recover the tank and Sgt. Vines' body. He found the tank batteries flat, and before he could start it he had to run the "homelite" (the small charging motor) for three-quarters of an hour. When the batteries were sufficiently up, he managed to get it going and bring it back to the gun position. There is no doubt that this achievement required incredible courage, as the road was by no means secure, with pockets of Germans still in the area.

II. THE ACTION WHEN THE REGIMENT WAS ATTACKED BY 9TH S.S. PANZER DIVISION IN AREA BEAULIEU-MAISONCELLES, 3RD AUGUST, 1944.

At 0245 hours 3rd August 1944 the Regiment, then just north of Le Tourneur, received orders to move forward to a gun area between Beaulieu and Maisoncelles. Reconnaissance parties had to be on the ground at first light, guns to move at 0600 hours.

The enemy were known to occupy some positions in the woods on the point 279 feature to the north. Montchamp was thought to be in our hands, but this proved to be untrue.

The location of our own forward troops was uncertain, beyond the fact that 2nd Irish Guards were in La Marvindiere. However, the Division were of the opinion that the area was safe.

Bernard Brassey was not at all happy on the situation, and immediately asked for protection for the reconnaissance parties and gun line, but this was refused by Division.

The reconnaissance parties led by him arrived on the position about 0630 hours, having had considerable difficulty in finding their way in the dark, as the road running east from St. Charles de Percy to point 175 could not be used owing to heavy enemy shelling, and they had to go round by Beaulieu, Le Desert, and then up to point 176.

"R" Battery was deployed in two fields, just south of the lane running from point 176 to Maisoncelles, "P" Battery in one large field just south of "R" Battery, with "Q" Battery just to the west of the triangular wood, R.H.Q. being in the rear. The country in which the Regiment was deployed was mainly made up of small fields, with banks varying from three to five feet high, and fairly thick hedges on top surrounding them. The lanes shown running from east to west were all sunken lanes with banks approximately six feet high on either side.

As soon as the gun positions were decided on, Cliff Noble ("Q" Battery) was sent back to St. Charles de Percy to meet the guns and to bring them up. On his way back with the guns he reported thirty enemy infantry moving south, who hid in an orchard at his approach. The reconnaissance party immediately sent out patrols, but they were unable to contact the enemy, though some sniping was reported.

As soon as the guns were in action, which was about 0845 hours, they became engaged on a number of targets, during which time battery captains reconnoitred out to their flanks and forward, "Q" Battery being responsible for the right flank, "P" Battery and "R" Battery the left flank. Dick Brisbourne ("P" Battery) went forward about 400 yards with a local O.P. On arriving at a suitable position (shown in *Appendix B*) he saw a Panther tank (marked "P") about 300 to 400 yards away. He immedi-

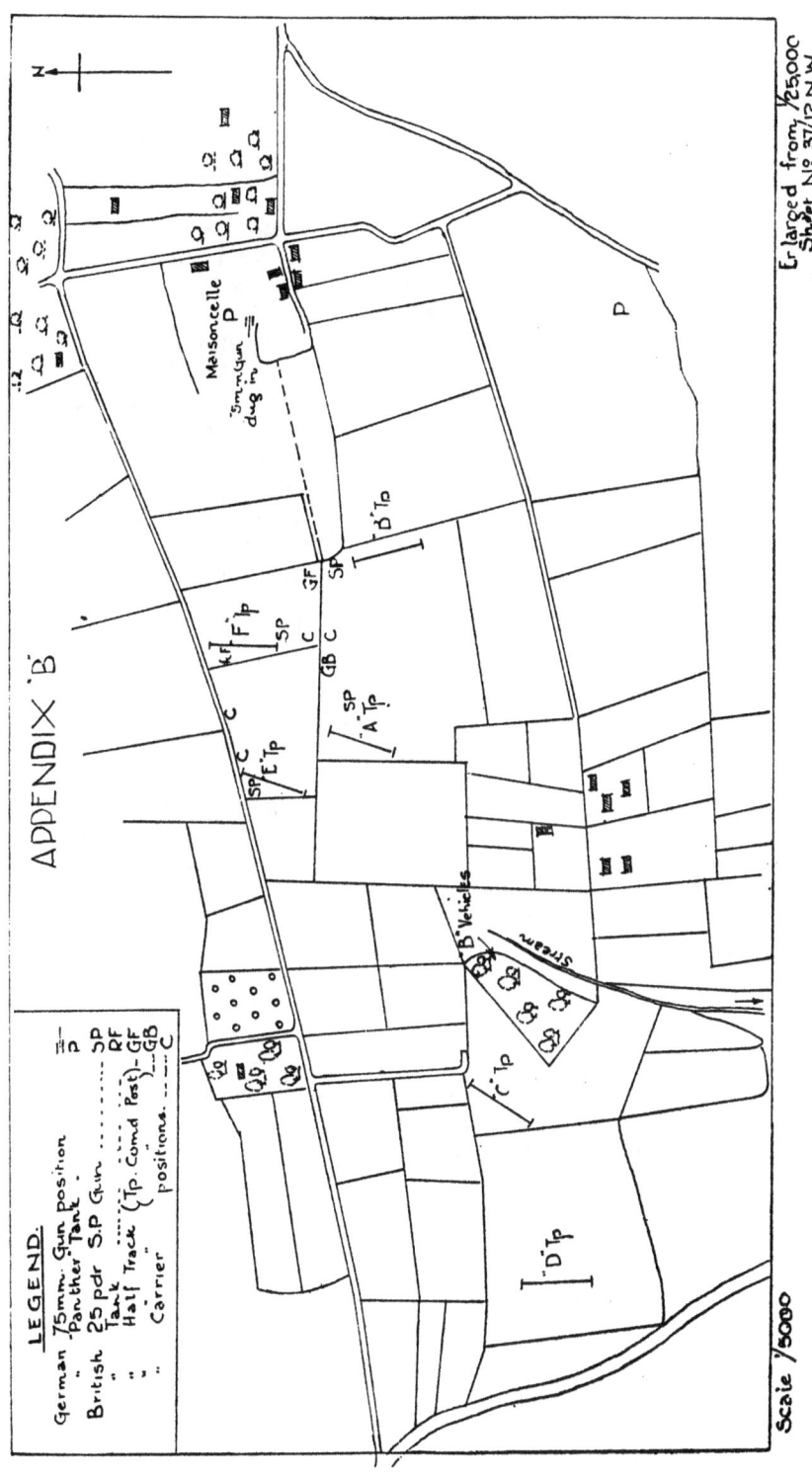

ately sent a runner back, to warn the Battery, who then sent up their tank R.B. The Panther, hearing the engines of the Sherman, then moved back into the lane to the S.E. of its original position. A few minutes later four more Panthers were reported moving up from the east towards "P" Battery's position, the original one moving round to join them at the same time.

Small-arms fire on to "P" Battery's position started at this moment, and appeared to come from the flanks and the front, a considerable amount being fired from trees overlooking the position. Sergeant Iliffe's gun, which was in the north-east corner of the field, was hit, and set on fire almost immediately by a dug-in 75-mm. (shown in *Appendix B*).

Fox Troop command post vehicle, which had broken down, and was just north of Sergeant Iliffe's gun, was next hit by the 75-mm. and set on fire. Shells then started to fall in the "E" Troop field, and the third shell hitting Sergeant Stearn's gun, which was in the N.W. corner of the field. German infantry were now reported moving up the lane on the left of "R" Battery's position, and were engaged by "F" Troop tank (Freddie Cawley), which was then in front of "F" Troop's guns. This tank next engaged a Panther, which was laying up to the 75-mm. but the results could not be observed. Owing to the turret jamming he had to withdraw behind the guns, and while doing so was hit broadside on, and set on fire. The whole crew escaped with slight burns. At this stage, heavy small arms fire was directed on to the Battery's position, and the order to retire came from R.H.Q. This order was sent over the wireless to both troops, but not received by Fox Troop, owing to their command post having been knocked out.

"E" Troop moved out, and Tony Ryder went over to Fox Troop and brought them out, having ordered one gun to fire a smoke screen to cover the withdrawal. During this period the right hand gun of Fox Troop (Sgt. Wilson) was hit and set on fire.

"P" Battery were engaging enemy infantry in the lane on their right, and to their left by firing H.E. into the trees in order to get air-burst effect. They got the order to withdraw shortly after "R" Battery, but "B" Troop did not receive the order owing to their command post having been knocked out. Dick Brisbourne, seeing "A" Troop moving out, then ordered "B" Troop to do the same. On the way out, the last S.P. (Sgt. Everard) was knocked out. R.B. Tank stayed behind to cover the Battery's withdrawal, Gnr. Brolly, the O.P.A. being in command. Donald Salt had led the soft vehicles round behind the battery, in an attempt to get them out by the triangular wood. Gaps through the banks had been made by the tanks, but unfortunately the leading vehicle, a water truck, became bogged, blocking the way, and eventually these vehicles had to be abandoned, after the ammunition truck had been hit by H.E. and blown up. In all, nine vehicles were lost here.

Meanwhile "Q" Battery on the right had been ordered to remain in action until the other batteries had withdrawn, and to cover the withdrawal as best as they could.

Their gun position by this time was coming in for considerable small-arms fire. "D" Troop having withdrawn, "C" Troop moved back into their position, and fired smoke and H.E. towards the triangular wood, from which small-arms fire was now coming, also there were some air bursts over the position, which appeared to come from the same place, probably fired by Panthers. This was subsequently borne out, by the fact that two Panthers were found "brewing up" between the original "C" Troop position and the triangular wood. "C" Troop then retired one gun at a time, the Battery Captain (Peter Winslow) and G.P.O. (Sam Hughes) coming out on the last gun. As this gun came off the position, so the first M.10 of "Q" Battery 21 A/Tank Regiment arrived. We are pleased to record that they subsequently killed five of the Panthers. Bob Clark, B.C., of "R" Battery, with Gnr. Gregory and L/Bdr. Smith, made two sorties, during the action, with a Piat. The first time he reached a point, down the lane on the north of the position, about 300 yards ahead of "F" Troop, where he had a shot at a Panther to his right, but it unfortunately dropped twenty yards short, although causing the Panther to withdraw before he was able to get in another shot.

The second time he went forward after the guns had retired, having given an order for a Piat to be brought to him. He got within twenty yards of a Panther near "A" Troop's old position, but had to retire before the Piat could be brought to him

The Regiment re-formed just east of Le Desert. Bernard Brassey was then ordered to reconnoitre a new gun area near La Terrerie. On the way back he and the Survey Officer ("Clarko") were heavily mortared on the crossroads at the bottom of the valley leading to La Terrerie, so decided to bring the Regiment in on a different route. Unfortunately, "Q" Battery took a track which petered out half-way up the southern slope of the hill just north of La Foueardiere, and while turning round in the field to come back, got heavily mortared by Nebelwerfers, and were lucky in having only four casualties (wounded), and one carrier destroyed. Peter Winslow managed to get the Battery out before any further fire could be brought to bear on them, as Nebelwerfers fortunately took about ten minutes to re-load, and stayed with B.S.M. Jackson, S/Sgt. Ash and Gnr. Sherring until the wounded could be evacuated.

The Regiment had not been long in its new position, when it was ordered back to its old one north of Le Tourneur.

There was yet one more blow to be borne, when the Padre, Archie Pryor, who had been with the Regiment since September 1939, was killed in Le Tourneur, by a shell which landed on the road just in front of his car. It was an exceptionally sad loss to the Regiment, for to all ranks at all times he had been such a good friend.

The total casualties suffered by the Regiment in this action were :—

Officers: The Padre, Rev. A. S. Pryor (killed); Capt. Hon. F. L. Cawley, Lieut. R. N. Leveson-Gower (both wounded) and Lieut. J. H. G. MacAlpine (missing).

N.C.O.s: W/O II F. D. Freer, Sgt. Corbett, Sgt. Wilson, Bdr. Hayes, Bdr. Harries, L/Bdr. Lund, L/Bdr. Gay, L/Bdr. Wakeling and Pte. Booth (attached R.A.S.C. D.R.) (all wounded).

Other Ranks: Gnr. Blaney, Gnr. Morgans, Gnr. Franks, Gnr. Wild, Gnr. Duxbury, Gnr. Thwaites, Gnr. Eggleton (all wounded); Gnr. Owen (missing, but later found killed); Gnr. Shaw (missing, but later re-joined); Gnr. Madden, Gnr. Noyes, Gnr. Pratt, Gnr. Dolman, Gnr. Withey (all missing); Gnr. Norton (missing, presumed killed).

Vehicles: 18 Wheeled Vehicles, 3 Motor Cycles, 1 Sherman Tank, 4 S.P. Guns, 6 Armoured Carriers, 2 Half-Tracks.

To end a bad day for the Regiment, the news came through that James Willoughby had been badly hurt whilst supporting the 2nd Irish Guards. He was helping an Officer of the 2nd Irish to get his "F" Echelon through to the position at La Marvindiere which had been cut off, and which was short of ammunition. He agreed with the officer that he should take care of a Panther which was crossing the road, and that he should dismount his .30 Browning, and spray up and down the road to get through.

As the column commenced to move a cloud of dust arose and the Germans mortared the road heavily. For protection he got himself under the Irish Guardsman's tank, who then unfortunately crossed a few yards to get a better view of the the Panther, and pinned James's legs under the track. As the engine was running, the tank commander could not hear James's cries, and an agonising twenty minutes followed while he lay with his feet pinned trying to give himself morphia and knowing all the time that the tank would reverse the length of the track before his legs would be free. Eventually this painful proceeding took place, and with the help of the M.O. of the 2nd Irish he was evacuated next morning. A letter received from him on the 14th August stated that he was in hospital at Worcester, and had great hopes of retaining his legs. Everyone hoped and prayed that this would prove to be the case, and wished him a speedy recovery.

The one really good feature of this black day was the work done by Bob Hoare and Luke Lillingston in support of the 1st and 2nd Battalions of Grenadier Guards. Major Rupert Bromley of the 1st Battalion wrote a very complimentary letter. As a result of the Regiment not being available during the majority of the day, it was necessary to give support to these battalions by other means. This was made possible through a "rep." of 63 Med., and also by calling on 55th Fd. Regt. through R.H.Q.

This worked out very well indeed, and the gist of Major Bromley's letter was that the artillery fire had been extremely prompt and accurate whenever called for throughout the day, when things had looked bad owing to enemy forming up for counter attacks, but the immediate response of the guns broke them all up.

III. END OF THE FIGHTING IN NORMANDY

During the next two days the Regiment remained in its position north of Le Tourneur, but on the 6th August it once more set off for St. Charles de Percy, and went into action there. Hostile shelling caused several casualties, forcing R.H.Q. to go to its alternative position. The following night, Lieut. T. Sherer, who had only been with us a few hours, was killed, and Sgt. Cullen died before he got back to the C.C.S. Sgt. Drew, Bdr. Wadsworth and Gnr. Wintle were wounded.

Padre March joined the Regiment here.

The following letter was received from Brigadier Phipps, C.R.A. on the 8th August, 1944:

"My dear Jock,

"Both the Corps Commander and General Allen have been most complimentary at the grand way my Div. Arty. have performed during the time we have been battling out here.

"I feel that the credit is due to my Regtl. Commanders, 2 I.C.s and B.C.s. They slaved hard in England, and in your case learned their new equipment and the manner of handling their O.P.s in a remarkably short time, and to such good effect that results have given our Armd. Bde. and 32 Bde. such confidence in your prowess that they rarely give you any rest.

"I am putting this on paper because I should like this to be a record of my appreciation of the efficiency of the Regiment, and I should be grateful if you'd let the remainder of your chaps know my pleasure in sending this to you.

Yours,

'Chink' "

On the 11th August the Regiment moved up to an area near Le Brien, and was in action there during some heavy fighting, during which the Division's losses were unfortunately rather heavy.

The Americans, since the beginning of the month, had swept south from Avranches, west into Brittany, and then east by Mayenne, to Argentan. Meanwhile, the Canadians struck south for Falaise.

These two drives threatened to encircle the German 7th Army, and to prevent this, the 922nd and 3/5 Para. Divisions fought violently on our Division front, especially round the Viessoix area. As a result of this, the Division was committed to very heavy fighting in bad country.

Alas, in this area, was lost one of the most liked officers the Regiment ever had, in Luke Lillingston. He was going forward to try and give support to the 1st Battalion Grenadier Guards, when his tank was hit, and caught fire immediately. He received bad burns and a nasty wound in the chest from which he died before getting back to the C.C.S. His loss was felt deeply by all who knew him. In action his coolness of mind was wonderful and his gameness superb. God rest his soul, and give him happy hunting.

After two or three days the Germans began to pull out, and the Division was gradually squeezed out from the fighting. It was very much hoped that orders would come to pursue them, but it was not to be. Instead, the Division was ordered to pull back and take up a proper defensive position, and for this the Regiment remained where it was.

As a result of casulaties, re-organisation was very necessary, and it was here that Chris Vesey arrived to command 129 Battery. Mike Townsend became "B" Troop Commander, as Bob Rowland Clark went to command 131 Battery. Other arrivals included Peter Studd to take over as Adjutant, Dick Bentley and Leslie

Yates to 131 Battery, Tony Baker and Campbell Reid to 130 Battery, and Mac Ross to 129 Battery.

In all, the Regiment sat down for about ten days, while the battle drifted further and further away. It was a great chance of doing a lot of maintenance, and becoming fully equipped again in tanks and S.P.s, and this time was vital, as was learnt later. Everyone was very glad too, to have a rest. There were those of course who couldn't, such as the vehicle mechanics who worked unceasingly, and the Q. Staff. As far as supplies were concerned, the whole onus of that side fell on the Quartermaster, Captain Vokins, and his team, who never failed to get all that was required.

Good news kept coming through—the Americans had gone right through Domfront and Alencon, and then there was the Falaise Gap victory, but still no orders to move came through.

It was a very pleasant time, with lovely weather, and glorious bathing near Beny Bocage. The only unpleasant job was that of burying the German dead, and the hundreds of cows killed in the battle, for which each Regiment had to send out working parties. The whole time was a complete anti-climax after the hard fighting.

On the 15th August the Corps Commander, with General Allen Adair, visited R.H.Q. and spoke to the Colonel, Bernard, and the three battery commanders. He spoke very highly of the Division, and the support that the artillery and the Regiment had given during the difficult fighting.

A lot of the officers went off on 24-hours sight-seeing tours, and some very pleasant visits were made to Rennes, Granville, Avranches, Mont St. Michael and the west coast. On the 21st August, the Colonel himself was ordered to take a two-days rest, and he went to a chateau at Tracy Bocage, which was set aside for officers for that purpose. He went in the very good company of Jim Lewis, who commanded the 2nd Bn. Welsh Guards, and enjoyed good food, papers, and a complete break from the battlefield which was so essential.

On the 23rd August came the news that Paris had been liberated. After a few days confused fighting, the scene was set again, the Americans through Marne, the advance through the south of France going well, and the remnants of the German 7th Army being liquidated west of the Seine.

On the 24th August orders to move at last came through —it was only that the Division would concentrate near Flers, but there was something in the air, and everyone felt that big things were afoot.

CHAPTER THREE

Pursuit through France and Fighting in Belgium

ON the 25th August the Regiment moved to its concentration area between Condé sur Noireau and Flers. R.H.Q. was in a very pleasant orchard and the batteries all close by. The little town of Condé had suffered the same fate as others, and was completely flat. Whilst here, a party from R.H.Q., including the Colonel, went up to the top of the nearby Mont de Cerisy, from which there was the most wonderful view, and it was obvious that the Germans must have seen the advance coming for miles. There was also a chateau there, privately owned before the war, but turned into a hospital by the Germans.

On the 28th August came the next move, and this time it was a long one, to a fresh concentration area at L'Aigle, which was about forty miles west of the Seine. It was a night move, with the tanks and S.P.s going on transporters. It was a nightmare move too, as it was pouring with rain and very dark. Dawn found the Regiment on a dreary road, soaked to the skin, and the first signs of the colossal damage done to the enemy transport in the Falaise battle were to be seen. Practically every hundred yards or so there was the wreckage of a German car or army truck.

The Divisional move itself had not taken place without its accidents, and, unfortunately, one of the 5th Brigade tanks attached to 130 Battery had gone over the edge of the road at a bend and completely overturned, with the transporter on top. Gnr. Richards and Gnr. Gillingham were with it, and the latter, who was in the tank commander's position at the time, was pinned underneath for five hours before he could be moved. He was extremely lucky to get away with a broken leg and slight injuries to his back.

The wheeled vehicles remained at L'Aigle for about twenty-four hours, but the transporters received fresh orders as they came along behind, to carry straight on past L'Aigle and go on up to the Seine.

One or two officers managed to take a jeep and pay a quick visit to the Falaise battlefield. All those who saw it will never forget in all their lives the awful scenes of death and destruction in that area. It certainly was a trap in which the Germans were properly caught, and everywhere was the wreckage of vehicles and tanks piled high on top of one another. Every lane leading east was choked with wreckage, and in so much of a hurry were the Germans to get away that many vehicles were telescoped into one another. There were thousands of prisoners burying their own dead, and also the cattle and horses which had suffered so terribly.

Mike Brown was staggered to find amongst the less damaged vehicles one of the 131 Battery armoured ammunition lorries which had been lost at Maisoncelles on the 3rd August. It had been repainted in the German camouflage colour, but it would not go. However, in his typical manner Mike took off his coat, rolled up his sleeves and got to work. He had a conscience about the way it was lost in the first place, and was determined somehow or other to make it go. He worked for hours with his fitters, getting completely covered in oil, but, alas, with a very crestfallen face, he had eventually to abandon the effort as the Germans had made too good a job of wrecking the engine.

The transporters stopped at Vernon, on the Seine, and the Regiment eventually re-grouped itself just on the other side of the river at about 0830 hours on the 30th August. It wasn't long before orders began to come through, and in an hour and a half the Regiment was once more on the move.

The Division had now been transferred to 30th Corps under Lieut.-General Horrocks, and the big plan was for an advance to be made by the Guards Armoured Division on the right, 8th Armoured Brigade in the centre, and 11th Armoured Division on the left. "An advance" is written because no one then knew what was to be accomplished. When the centre lines were given out, they made everyone fairly gasp.

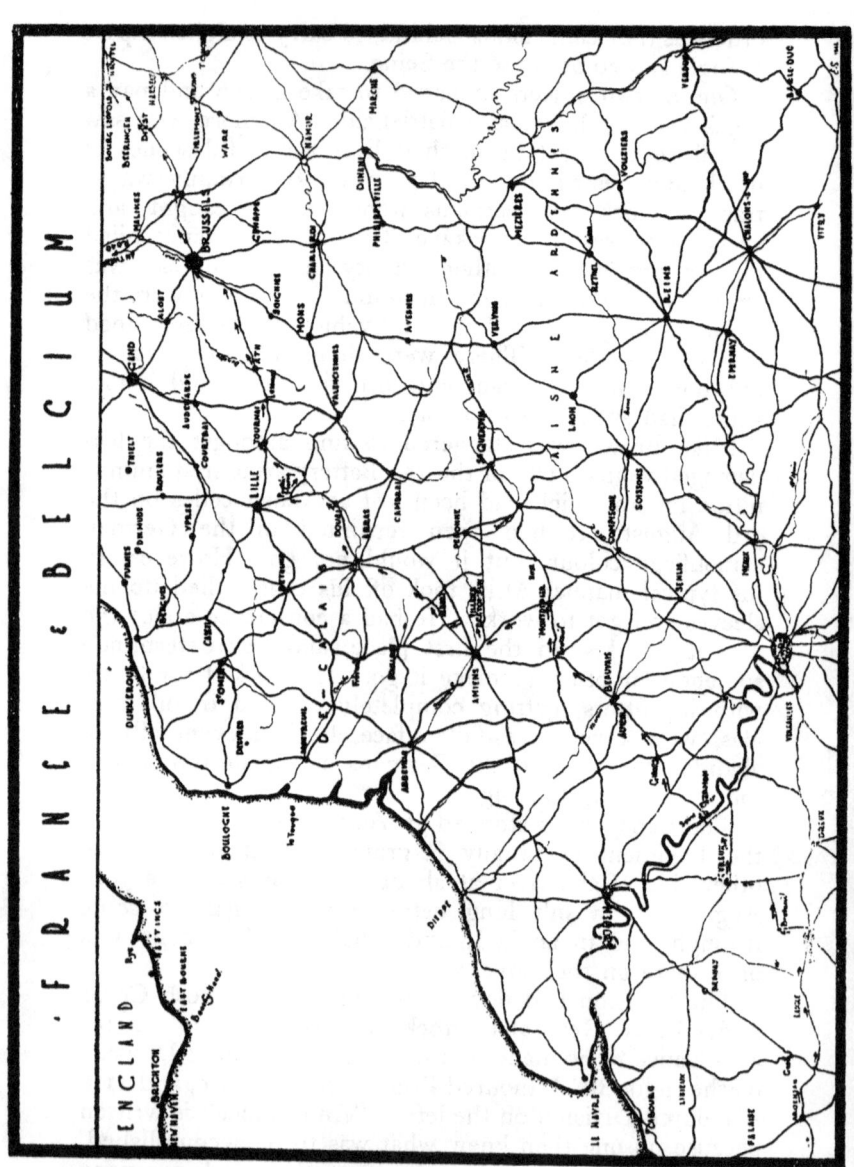

The Division's final objective was Brussels, with an intermediate bound on the Somme.

The reconnaissance troops of the Division had failed to find any trace of the enemy as far as Gisors, so at 1000 hours the chase started. The weather was frightful, and the rain was coming down in torrents, but, quite undeterred, the vehicles kept moving, and by nightfall the Regiment was north of Gisors. A small amount of opposition was met near Anneuil, but this was by-passed. At about midnight everyone was thinking about sleep, but this was not to be, and at 0230 hours the Regiment was on the move again.

It was south of Beauvais when dawn came, and later on that morning, after a halt for some breakfast, the town was passed through with the people giving everyone a wild welcome.

It is quite impossible to record the extraordinary contrast this moving chase was to the frightful slogging battles, and the awful scenes of death and destruction that everyone had got so used to in Normandy. To see beautifully clean streets, undamaged towns and villages, all filled with cheering civilians, and to be pelted with fruit and flowers, and in many cases wine too, was something far more than a mere thrill. There were of course one or two unpleasant scenes, such as women collaborators with their heads shaved, and the 130 Battery O.P.s with the Grenadiers even saw one completely stripped being marched through the streets.

The Intelligence Staff at Division had for the past week or so been preaching that the enemy would make a stand on the Somme.

It certainly appeared to be their intention from the few aerial photographs that were received, as there were signs of recent digging everywhere. This intention incidentally was confirmed later on by the German General in charge of the defence who was captured.

It was during the afternoon of 31st August, with the Grenadier Group and 130 Battery leading, that the Somme was reached at Corbie. The final objective of the day was the high ground on the other side of the river, and in case of any opposition the Regiment was deployed near an Australian war memorial at Villers Bretonneux to cover the crossing. There were in fact a few Germans who were fighting, but they were quickly overcome.

It was during this day, and for the rest of the chase in France, that many contacts were made with the Maquis. They were everywhere along the route, in small groups, and most of them armed with captured German rifles. They were all wild with joy at the rapid advance, and mad-keen to do anything to help, and to come to grips with the Germans. Sometimes over enthusiastic, they gave false information, as with one amusing incident that happened to 130 Battery on that day.

It was during one of the few long halts that the Regiment had, that they said they knew that a wood not far from the road had a lot of Germans hiding inside, who would not give themselves up. As it was easy to deploy in that spot, Bernard Brassey, who had been approached, turned two of 130 Battery guns on to the wood, and they blasted it with everything they had got for about five minutes, expecting the Germans to come marching out swiftly with their hands in the air. But no, not a bit of it, instead, a herd of wild boar, and so astonished were the Battery who were looking on, that those with rifles and especially Bob Eady, the B.S.M., forgot all their rules of aiming, and not a single boar was put in the bag!

The Maquis were extremely useful in looking after prisoners. In such a swift advance, with such a demoralised enemy, it could easily have been the most serious of problems. The Germans were giving themselves up in their hundreds, and the Division must have accounted for thousands during the chase. As it was, as soon as they came in (and what dejected, ragged, dirty and unhappy looking specimens they were too) they were given to the nearest Maquis, and there was nothing more to worry about! They were always delighted to take them, and looked after them most effectively!

The Regiment stayed the night of 31st August south of the Somme, but was pushing on again across the river by 0600 hours the next day. The objective was Neuville, near Arras, and although there were rather more enemy about, they were in no more heart to fight than on the

129 Battery near Douai

"The Times" Photograph

Bridge over River at Nijmegen

D.U.K.W.s moving up to the River

previous day. At the end of the afternoon, the Colonel and Bernard Brassey were doing a reconnaissance to find a position for the Regiment, when they came across the Colonel's tank crew with Charlie Helps rounding up about thirty Germans. It was certainly an amusing sight to see the Colonel standing over them on guard with a rifle, whilst the second-in-command disarmed them! They had several most useful vehicles with them, which of course were immediately taken on strength, and one was a sort of mobile kitchen which also had in it an excellent supply of pork chops. Gnr. Goodwin, the Colonel's batman, was very displeased at having to march the prisoners back down the road!

But this was one of many similar incidents, and each battery collected a good bag for the day. The Germans could often be seen in large batches on a slope away from the road, waiting as it seemed for someone to arrive to take them away. When the arrival was announced by a shell somewhere near, up went their hands as if one man, and in they came.

The next day, 2nd September, the Regiment advanced to Douai, arriving in the early afternoon. The Irish Group were leading, and the whole Division harboured on the airfield, which, apart from demolitions on the runways, appeared to be fairly intact. There was no more moving for that day, and at once everyone got down to the very necessary maintenance required on the tanks and S.P.s.

Late that night the orders came through for the next day, and little did anyone know what a day it was to be. The objective was Brussels, nearly a hundred miles ahead, and on the left the 11th Armoured Division was to capture Antwerp. The operation was to be combined with an airborne landing, but at the eleventh hour this was cancelled owing to bad weather, and, as it turned out, of course it was not needed.

Within the Division a great race was organised, as it was to move on two centre lines, 5th Brigade on the left, and 32nd Brigade on the right. The Regiment, working with the Coldstream and Grenadier Groups, was on the left, and from the map it looked the more difficult route, having many more small cross-country roads to move on than the other.

The advance started at about 0700 hours on the 3rd September, and for a while all went well. Everyone was suffering from liberation fever, and at a village called Pontaumarq the Grenadiers, who were leading, were brought up with a very sharp jolt when one minute they were doing their best to catch the apples and flowers that were being thrown at them, and the next they were being pelted by 88-mms. from some Germans. The enemy pocket provided quite a tough nut to crack, and 130 Battery had to deploy, and Campbell-Reid did two shoots for the Grenadiers. However, when the situation was well in hand, Brigadier Norman wisely decided to by-pass them and push-on, leaving a company group to mop up the pocket of Germans of which about a hundred prisoners were taken.

The Belgian frontier was passed about 1215 hours, and Tournai was entered soon after. The Belgian reception in the towns was even greater than the French, and everywhere was seen the Belgian flag waving and being waved by the thousands.

The next town was Lessines, where a whole column of horse-drawn German transport had been completely wiped out by the leading troops, and was one of the worst sights ever seen. The inhabitants, who had been in short supply of meat, were already carving them up, and the contents of the waggons had been scattered all over the streets.

In the early afternoon the Household Cavalry reconnoitering out in front, reported a clear road, except for minor opposition, to the capital, and everyone pushed on as hard as they could. Every so often, to try everyone's patience there were halts as this opposition was met, but it was always overcome fairly quickly, and smouldering German lorries, and prisoners, were continually being seen.

It was growing dark when the Regiment turned into the road where the trams for Brussels started. The tanks and vehicles must have been going at a steady 30 m.p.h. as the column swept through the suburbs of the city. The crowds were in their thousands, and surged forward as the vehicles went by, really quite frightening for the drivers.

But this speed could not last, and as the crowds grew greater so the speed slowed down, until it was impossible to go faster than a walking pace. The scenes inside the city were indescribable, and it will be impossible ever to forget them. Red, black and yellow fluttered from every window, and was worn on coats and dresses. Bonfires of Nazi literature and German notices were burning at every street corner, and people were dancing wildly in the streets, singing "Tipperary."

The blackout was completely disregarded, as all the cafes and houses were brilliantly lit, and in some streets floodlights were even turned on to the vehicles.

Eventually, it was almost impossible to move at all, and if any one stopped to ask the way, or got out of his vehicle, he was immediately set upon by the seething crowd, signs were torn from his battledress, and he received at least a hundred kisses. Every vehicle was completely snowed under with the fruit and wine, beer and champagne, that was thrown in from every direction, and there were many painful bruises as a result.

Finally, the Regiment arrived outside the Chateau Royale at about midnight, although it was a complete mystery how it ever got there complete. R.H.Q. became involved with three German lorries full of men trying to make their get-away and it looked as though it had the makings of a first-class street battle, but very soon they were rounded up and marched off by the Belgian police.

Standing at the gates of the palace was the Queen Mother, and the welcome and thanks she gave to the many officers and men who shook hands with her was really touching. The crowds still stayed on, even when everyone was preparing for sleep and making their beds on the pavement.

Getting up the next morning was just the same, and many were awakened by people from the crowds with cups of coffee and tea! They still stayed whilst everyone got up, dressed, washed and shaved!

The Regiment of course was hoping for a twenty-four hours stay, and a night-out in the city, but there was a job to be done and it was not to be. No one was allowed to go into the town, and at one o'clock orders came through that the Grenadier Group with 130 Battery should advance and capture Louvain, and they left soon after. The airfield outside the capital was heavily defended by 88-mms. but another route was taken, and these were successfully by-passed. As a precaution, the rest of the Regiment was deployed opposite the Chateau Royale, where they could reach the airfield, but there was no trouble. They subsequently cleared off during the night.

A lot of prisoners were taken at Louvain by the Grenadiers, and Bob Hoare and Derek Baer did a lot of chasing and rounding up on the outskirts.

On the 6th September the Divisional advance continued, and was headed towards the Albert Canal. It became apparent early on that the galloping advance up to Brussels would not continue, and that the Germans were determined to make a stand on this formidable water obstacle. The Regiment went into action near Tessenderloo, where it stayed overnight. The next day, information came through that an enemy force including fifty tanks was expected at Diest, and so the Regiment moved south to meet this threat, but nothing materialised.

Meanwhile the Welsh Guards had forced a crossing over the canal at Beeringen. The Germans of course had blown all the bridges, but this one they had not made a very good job of, and was repairable.

On the 8th September the Division crossed, and the Regiment went into action on the other side. It was not a pleasant spot, and was shelled practically every night. However, everyone was well dug in, and although there were many shell-holes dotted around amongst the guns, there were few casualties. Amongst the few, unfortunately, was Mike Brown and all his vehicle crew, who were wounded, and a newly-joined officer called Pearson, also wounded. It was heard later that Mike subsequently died of his wounds. He was a great loss to 131 Battery and to the Regiment. No one worked harder than he did for the good of the cause.

Orders for the 11th September were very unpleasant. The Division was to advance towards the next water obstacle, the Escaut Canal, by-passing Hechtel which was

ALBERT & L'ESCAUT CANALS

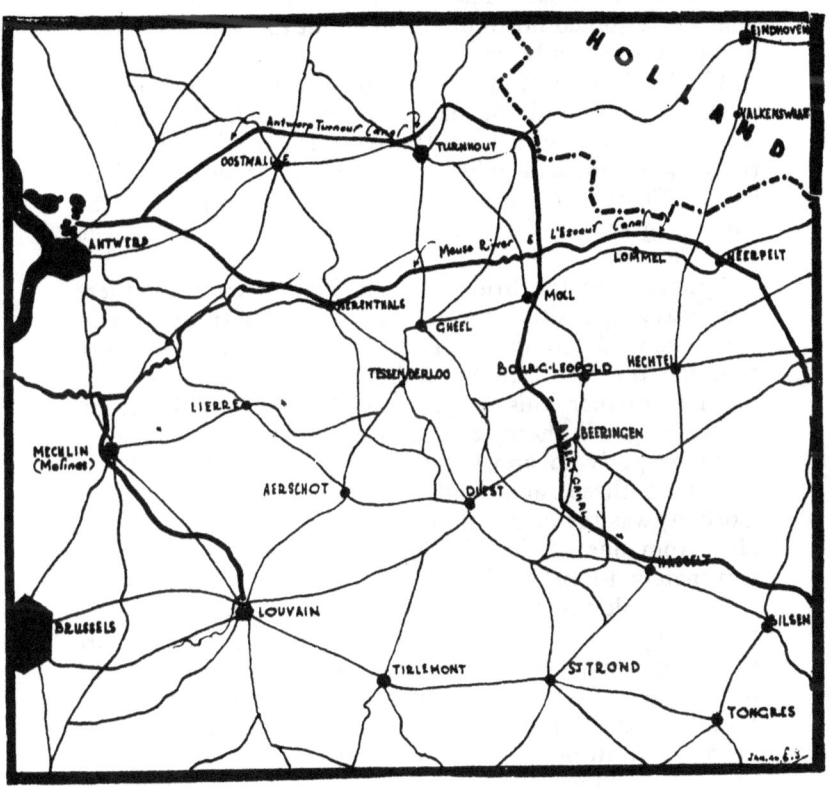

strongly held by the Germans. The Welsh Guards were heavily involved here with 129 Battery, but the rest of the Division was being used to go cross-country in the advance. Bourg-Leopold was also strongly held to the left, and the plan was for the Irish and Grenadier Groups to go in between. The Regiment moved up to support them at 0400 hours, and went into action just south of the road adjoining the two towns. There was a big fire plan, and the Regiment did a lot of shooting, including a smoke screen to the flank. The advance went well, and centre line was re-joined north of Hechtel, but the going was very heavy in the sandy soil.

The land in point of fact was the artillery range for the Belgian Army, and the day was very much like a firing exercise on Larkhill, with the batteries continually leap-frogging ahead, and only staying in a position for a short time. There is no doubt that, as it was a bad going, the support given to the battalions would never have been possible without the S.P.s.

Approaching the bridge on the Eindhoven road, there was heavy opposition met about two miles short of it in very wooded country. There were several 88-mms. covering the direct route, and it was impossible to push on any further this way. The Regiment did several "mike targets" there, but it was impossible to observe them properly to knock them out. Campbell Reid was observing these, and whilst doing so, his driver, Gnr. Corbett, was hit in the chest by an airburst shell, presumably from one of the 88 mms., a wound which was unfortunately to prove fatal.

Meanwhile the Irish Guards found another route round to the right, and by a brilliant coup managed to capture the bridge intact, and formed a small bridgehead on the other side. At the same time, another route round was found by the Grenadiers, who shot up the troublesome 88-mms. from behind, and so great was the damage done that it was impossible to move down the road because of the burning German equipment.

The next morning, before dawn, the Regiment moved up expecting the advance to continue, but soon heard that there was going to be a halt of several days before it would, as the supply situation was getting rather behind-hand, and not at all to be wondered at.

The Regiment deployed to cover the bridgehead, but not a great deal of shooting was done. What there was, was out towards Lommel, to the left of the area, where several good shoots were done on German transport endeavouring to get back over the canal.

Maintenance was the order of the day, and there were one or two parties as well, to try out the champagne captured in the large store that the Germans left behind in Brussels.

On the 13th September, Lieut.-General Horrocks, the Corps Commander, came to R.H.Q. and saw the Colonel, Bernard Brassey, Bob Hoare, Chris Vesey, Bob Rowland Clark and Peter Studd. He was most complimentary, and was greatly liked, and his visit very much appreciated.

Peter Studd now took over the full duties of Adjutant, and Tony Tasker went back to command "D" Troop. Derek Baer took over "C" Troop, and Campbell Reid went to 131 Battery.

Soon afterwards it was heard that big things were in the air for the next operation, and as it was well known that an airborne army had been waiting for some time in England for the right moment to come for its use, it was felt that they would be seen very soon, and so it turned out to be.

CHAPTER FOUR

Fighting in Holland and the First Glimpse of Germany

I. BATTLE FOR NIJMEGEN.

The push into Holland was organised for the 17th September, and planned in conjunction with the greatest airborne operation of the war. Two American airborne divisions were to drop and capture intact all the main bridges between Eindhoven and Nijmegen, and the British 1st Airborne Division was to drop at Arnhem. 30th Corps, with the Guards Armoured Division leading, was to advance and make contact as quickly as possible. At 1300 hours the first flight of Dakotas could be seen on the horizon, followed shortly afterwards by hundreds of others, and at 1400 hours the Regiment moved off behind the Irish Group, which was leading the attack.

It was very slow going, as the Germans had had plenty of time to organise their defences, and there were many 88-mms. concealed in the wooded country. But there was terrific artillery support being given by an A.G.R.A., and also rocket-firing Typhoons. By nightfall the leading troops had just managed to reach Valkenswaard, while the Regiment harboured in pouring rain on the side of the road just south of the town and just beyond a grim place where eight Irish Guards tanks were still burning.

The Regiment moved again at first light, but by mid-day it had still not cleared the town, in fact it had to go into action on the outskirts, firing on troops the other side. It remained here during the afternoon, firing concentrations the whole time, until just as darkness was approaching, when it appeared that the opposition had been overcome. The Regiment had to come out of action very quickly, and the whole Division pushed on as hard as they could in the dark.

Eindhoven was passed through between 2200 and 2300

hours, where there were terrific crowds cheering and waving, and at every small river crossing there were American paratroops who had done a grand job of work in capturing them intact. Unfortunately they were just too late at the bridge over the Wilhelmina Canal at Zon, and a halt was called just south of the blown bridge, and the Regiment went into harbour. The R.E.s worked flat out all through the night and did very well to get it completed by first light. An amusing incident happened that night when a certain gunner officer walked on to the bridge to see how it was progressing, when a German prisoner who was helping in the job turned and spoke to him in perfect English and told him to move off as he was "bloody well getting in everybody's way and holding up the work!" He was not in the Regiment!

On the 19th the move again started at first light and, with the Grenadier Group and 130 Battery leading, it was for a time a "Covent Garden" march, with fruit and flowers being pelted at the battery from every direction. The magnificent bridge at Grave had been captured intact, but on the other side the situation was obscure. Contact was eventually made with the paratroops on the high ground south of Nijmegen, who had captured this, but the town and bridge remained in enemy hands.

General Browning, commanding the Airborne Corps, had already set up his H.Q., and he thought that the enemy had no guns bigger than 40-mm., and thought it might be possible to rush the bridge with a troop of tanks, but it was soon found that the opposition was of a very different nature. The Regiment went into action three miles south of the town, at Malden, and a plan was formed between the Americans and the Grenadiers. There ensued a lot of very heavy and difficult street fighting near the bridge and by the roundabout, and also round the Post Office from which it was believed that the switch to blow up the bridge might operate. The infantry wanted a smoke screen to be put across the river on each side of the bridge, but this was obviously not possible, and instead a target was selected, being the area on the far side of the bridge. The plan was for the Regiment to fire on this for three minutes at intense rate prior to the assault being put in. Although it fired on it many times the Grenadiers were never able to get quite to it, and the attack had to be called off until the next day.

Throughout the 20th September the Regiment remained in the same location. It was on that morning that the sad news of the death of Tony Tasker was reported. He was in a house near the bridge which was also being used by an American mortar O.P., and the room he was observing from got a direct hit from a shell. He and his crew, Bdr. May, Bdr. Ashwell and Gnr. Chamberlain, had done really splendid work with the Americans, having had a most unpleasant time being continually shelled and mortared. No worse loss could have been sustained by the Regiment. His crew carried on and supported the Grenadiers and Americans, and did several very good shoots, until relieved later on in the day. He was buried that evening in an orchard near the guns.

Later on in the afternoon it was decided to launch the troop of Grenadier tanks and rush the bridge. The Regiment fired smoke and H.E. concentrations at the same time to cover the airborne troops crossing the river west of the town. By this means the bridge was captured intact about 1700 hours, and troops were immediately sent across to form a bridgehead. The bridge was soon to be known as Grenadier Bridge, but it subsequently transpired that during the previous night a Dutch boy in the resistance movement had crawled along the edge of the bridge and cut all the wires in the demolition boxes, and the bridge is now named after him. He crossed over the next day with the first of the Grenadier tanks, but was unfortunately killed.

At about 1800 hours 131 Battery were ordered to turn their guns round and support some infantry who were attacking south of Nijmegen near a village called Wyler, and with the first target taken on, "C" Sub of "E" Troop, ranging, they were the first shells from British field guns to fire into Germany during this war.

Early next morning the Regiment was ordered to move on over the bridge, 129 Battery moving first, supporting the Irish Group who were leading the attack. The general plan was to push on as hard as possible and relieve the 1st British Airborne in Arnhem, who were now in desperate straits, having had severe casualties, and who were now running short of food and ammunition.

After a short deployment in some allotments just outside the town, the remainder of the Regiment crossed the bridge at about lunch-time. The traffic got into an awful jam, and it was actually just as 130 Battery was on the bridge that the column could move no further. The bridge was a wonderful sight and one that will be remembered by all who saw it that day. It was quite obvious that with the number of German aircraft flying round in circles overhead and the sporadic shelling attempts by the enemy it would be unwise to stay there too long, so by double, and even triple, banking on the far side all the Regiment's vehicles and S.P.s were cleared from the bridge itself.

Whilst waiting on the far side, 130 Battery received information from the H.C.R. that a church was a suspected O.P. in Bemel, and as this could be seen from where they were, Bob Hoare turned his guns round on the road and took it on over open sights, having the great satisfaction shortly afterwards in seeing it blown up. At the same time "A" Troop of the 94th Light A.A. were shooting furiously at all the German planes, and a great deal of the credit must go to them for the two Messerschmidts that were shot down that afternoon. They always supported the Regiment with their guns and were always absolutely splendid.

Just as it was getting dark, the Regiment deployed all round the northern part of the bridge, in very cramped and not at all desirable positions, but all that was available. Meanwhile, 43rd Division had been ordered to go through and clear the way to Arnhem and relieve the 1st British Airborne. Unfortunately, this was never achieved, in spite of every effort and dropping of more Polish paratroops. Nevertheless, the H.C.R. did a great job in finding a route round by the western side to the Neder Rhine, and it is history now that the remnants of the Division were withdrawn on this route.

On the 22nd September the Regiment fired on targets intermittently in support of the 43rd Division. The

Germans in turn were mortaring and shelling the area round the northern end of the bridge. 130 Battery were very unfortunate in having a complete load of Nebelwerfers to land right in their battery position, which was in the garden of a hospital. Doug. Hamilton and his signaller were both killed, and Gnr. Ames of "D" Troop was badly wounded. They had all done extremely well and were a very great loss.

In the afternoon it was learned that the centre line had been cut by Germans moving east near Veghel, and the Grenadier Group, with 130 Battery in support, were ordered back to clear it up. They moved back in the evening, and shortly afterwards the remainder of the Regiment was ordered back to its former position in the allotments south of the river.

The next day it was ordered to move again, and it joined 130 Battery just north of Uden to support the Grenadier Group. The centre line was cleared during the day after some very confused fighting. Derek Baer did some very good shoots in the late afternoon, silencing the German light flak guns which were firing at the Dakotas and Stirlings which were pouring over bringing supplies to the airborne forces. After the targets had been correctly ranged on, they were taken on every time the planes appeared, and it gave great satisfaction to see them come over and have a clear passage.

The 24th and 25th September were spent patrolling, but on the 26th the 32nd Brigade, then consisting of the Grenadier and Coldstream Groups, was ordered to clear the west flank of the centre line at Heesch and Oss and to guard the large food dump at the latter. The Regiment moved north to support this attack, and went into action between Grave and Heesch. This attack took up the days until the 30th, the Regiment moving forward gradually the whole time as the range became too great. It fired a very great number of rounds both by day and night, and once completely broke up a counter-attack started by the Germans. A great number of prisoners were taken, who were very dazed and shaken, and who testified to the accuracy of the shooting. Meanwhile, the 7th Armoured Division had all the time been advancing from the south-east and gradually took over the front to advance on s'Hertogenbosch.

Late on the 30th September, just as everyone was expecting to be able to get some rest and have some time for maintenance, information came through that the Americans were expecting a big attack to come in from the south-east directed at the bridge in Nijmegen. In point of fact 130 Battery were fortunate, as they stayed behind to rest with the Grenadiers in Grave, but the remainder of the Regiment with the Coldstream Group moved that evening to the south-east of Nijmegen. It was not a pleasant spot, as there was a good deal of shelling and bombing, mostly by night. Sometimes the Regiment supported the Americans and sometimes the 43rd Division troops north of the river, with the result that the guns were continually having to alter their zero-lines. 129 Battery experienced most of the shelling, but the Regiment was fortunate in having no casualties, and it was with great relief that orders came to pull out on 4th October and to go down to the 130 Battery area, near Grave, and rest.

The period between 4th and 12th October was spent there. Everyone went off to cinema and ENSA shows and baths in Nijmegen, which were badly needed. A really excellent Divisional Club was opened in Grave Barracks and most of the officers were fortunate enough to have a short stay in Brussels. On the 11th October it was learned that the Regiment would have to relieve the Herts. Yeomanry (86th Field Regiment, R.A.) who had beforehand relieved this Regiment in support of the 82nd Airborne Division south-east of Nijmegen, and this meant going back to the country which was beginning to be well known.

Before the move, however, on the 12th His Majesty the King visited the area, and a parade was held in Grave Barracks in which the Colonel was presented ; Bernard Brassey, Bob Hoare and eighteen other ranks of the Regiment attended at the time.

At about mid-day, Brigadier Norman Gwatkin called the parade to attention whilst the King walked round and talked to each Commanding Officer. He said he had heard that the Leicestershire Yeomanry had done very good work in support of his Guards Armoured Division.

During this period Jerry Green arrived to take over the duties of "D" Troop Commander, and also Jack Smith and Jock McKenna who had spent three rather annoying months in R.H.U.s. They both went to 131 Battery.

By the end of the 13th October the Regiment was deployed and well dug-in on the high ground south-east of Nijmegen. Where possible, command posts were put near farms and houses to get the maximum of comfort.

130 Battery were unlucky in their position, for early in the morning the enemy started ranging on the only house on their position and did a copybook pin-point target, finally scoring a direct hit. Unfortunately they had one casualty as a result, one of the ranging rounds wounding Sergeant Ellis, who had to have a leg amputated. The Battery quickly moved to an alternative position after this. R.H.Q. took over a liaison H.Q. at H.Q.R.A. 82nd U.S. Airborne Division, known as Channel Command Post. The Colonel acted as British C.R.A. and the fire of the artillery of the Guards Armoured Division, 43rd Division, 5th A.G.R.A. and the American guns was all co-ordinated from this H.Q. The one thing that was most striking was the absolute first-class efficiency of the American communication. Both their telephone installations and their wireless sets, which were crystal, were far better than the British. They never seemed to have any difficulty in getting through and the words, "say again" were never spoken.

The American C.R.A. was 49-years old, and had been in all the drops that the Division had undertaken; Africa, Sicily, Anzio, Normandy and now this latest one, a really fine record. Lieut.-Colonel Griffiths and Lieut.-Colonel Smiley were two equally pleasant and efficient officers, and they were all billeted in Leicester, Market Harborough, Hinckley and various villages prior to coming over. With one accord they seemed very grateful for the hospitality shown to them.

Altogether the Regiment remained in this position until 10th November, supporting the Americans, but as things were fairly quiet it was possible to pull one battery out at a time for a rest of about a week. 130 Battery were the first to come out and they went into billets in Malden. It did everyone a lot of good, and, for the first time since leaving England, every single man slept under cover. They went back into action on the 26th, and 131 Battery then came out, and after that 129 Battery. It was the same to all three, the Dutch were very kind and gave everyone, officers and men alike, a very good time.

On the 15th the Regiment fired its first propaganda shoot! The pamphlets were placed in smoke shells, replacing the smoke, and the papers were shot out of the base in the same way. They were written in German and Polish and were specially directed to the German 84th Division which was known to be on the front. Only known results were nine prisoners! Before the Regiment left this front there were two other propaganda shoots, but from these no known results were ever heard.

On the 16th proper arrangements were made by Divisional H.Q. for sending personnel on leave to Brussels and Antwerp. But the allotment was very small and only a few were lucky.

As many officers and senior N.C.O.s as possible attended a conference at Grave held by the Corps Commander, who gave a most splendid account of the battle that the Division had been through under his command, and gave a very good idea of the prospects for the future.

On the 22nd the regimental soccer team had a match against the "Micks"—2nd Bn. Irish Guards—on the Stadium Ground at Nijmegen. It was a match that had been looked forward to, as it had been put off several times the previous winter in Yorkshire. At half-time the score was 1—1, but after that the "Micks" improved, and in a first-class open game the Regiment lost 1—3. Two other good matches were played, against 21st A/Tank Regiment, R.A., and Divisional Signals, both of which we won.

On 6th November a very successful regimental dance was held in the Winter Gardens at De Veereeniging. A large proportion of the Regiment attended and it was greatly enjoyed. The shortage of girls was inevitable, but the ladies hockey teams (Quick Club) turned up in strength, and very nice girls they were too, besides being first-class hockey players, to which the regimental officers' hockey team will testify, being on one occasion beaten by them in spite of the Major's agility at back! It all seemed so strange actually coming away from the Regimental position, quite possibly with shells being thrown over, to participate in either football or hockey, or go to a dance, and then back into the position with the Germans a few thousand yards away.

During this long spell the administrative side of R.H.Q. was near the Holy Land Institute—very wonderful mosaics and reproductions of scenes in the life of Our Lord. The Father Superior gave up a room in his house, he was called Van Beck and was very kind, very much of the chosen race and quite an interesting but sly old fox, and no one ever knew quite how much he could be trusted.

On 3rd November the Divisional Commander arrived to see the Regiment in action, and walked round the guns afterwards having lunch at R.H.Q. He was extremely interested and pleased in everything that he saw, especially in the cleverly built dug-outs, in the construction of which everyone was now becoming very skilled. They nearly all had proper doorways leading into them, electric light and fireplaces, and later on some even had wooden bunks as well.

At the end of October the Regiment heard that the next big push was to take place from Nijmegen, going south-east into Germany. A large dumping programme was put in hand, and in two days hundreds of rounds per gun were placed in the Regiment's alternative position and carefully camouflaged. It sounded as if it was to be a very big show, with the Divisional tanks helping in the initial barrage. But it came to nothing and all the plans were changed. All the ammunition had to be taken away, and the Division was to move to the Aachen sector, with the Canadians taking over at Nijmegen. The weather, which had deteriorated rapidly in the past week, was possibly the cause of the cancellation, and everywhere in the gun positions one had to walk about in a foot of mud. It certainly would not have been possible for tanks to go across-country.

Railway Bridge at Nijmegen (The Span was bombed by Stukas the day after the Regiment arrived)

Leading Tank of 2nd Irish Guards, knocked out in attempt to reach Arnhem

R.H.Q. Officers at Halmael

II. MOVE INTO GERMANY.

The reconnaissance parties under Bernard Brassey moved down to the new area on the 10th November, and by this time it was heard that the Division would take part of the front held by the Americans in the Sittard area. Nobody was really sorry to get away from the very wet and boggy area, for however well a dug-out is built, it gets very damp and monotonous after a while.

The hand-over to the Canadian Artillery was completed by the 11th, and for that night the Regiment had once again very comfortable billets on the Nijmegen-Venlo road. The move down to Sittard took place the next day. All went well as far as Eindhoven, but after that it began to pour with rain, the traffic was awful, and with very big halts because of it the Meuse was not crossed at Berg until nearly midnight. The night was spent by the whole Regiment in an enormous barn full of some by-product from a chemical factory in Geleen. It was so big that it could have almost housed another Regiment as well.

The next morning the Regiment moved at once to the positions prepared for it by the reconnaissance party. R.H.Q. and 131 Battery were in Germany at a little village called Hillensberg, and 129 and 130 Battery were in Holland at Jabeek, except for one gun of "C" Troop which was just over the border. The Grenadier Group had taken over the front, and it was grand to be back supporting the Guards Armoured Division again.

It was very strange being in Germany. A completely different atmosphere reigned everywhere, and the farms and their workers might have been ghosts. There was no trouble at all from the population, but just in case, a very strict curfew was imposed, and there was no shortage of sentries. There was no thought of malicious looting or anything like that, but at the same time there was every reason why the men should make themselves as comfortable as possible, and with this end in view a great number of tables and chairs were removed from the houses.

Soon after the Regiment arrived all the inhabitants (except thirty-five to look after the animals) from the area just inside Germany were evacuated, and the day after that all the animals went. The cattle were most unruly and greatly resented being taken from the Fatherland. A swastika medal was found in one house which had been presented to a German woman for bearing an illegitimate child by a German soldier. What an extraordinary mentality they have!

Very soon everyone began to grow fat due to the excellent supplementary rations left behind by the Germans, in goose, pork and veal! Every house had a cellar, and every cellar was full of hundreds of bottles of fruit which made a delightful change to the everlasting 14-man pack rations.

The Regiment had three O.P.s deployed, 129 Battery at Kievelburg, 130 Battery at Vintelen and 131 Battery at Hastenrath, each supporting their own battalions. The battalions only had a squad or company group out at a time, which changed round every few days. Practically all the battery officers took a turn at manning their O.P.s, and there was always something to do, as the Germans could be plainly seen just over the valley, and every now and then some digging party would be "hotted up." However, there was plenty of retaliatory firing by the enemy, and all three O.P.s came in for a great deal of mortaring and shelling, fortunately suffering no casualties.

The Signal Section had to work extremely hard, and so did the battery signallers. Conditions were absolutely apalling, with mud far worse than anything yet experienced, and it was quite impossible to move anywhere except by jeep or carrier. Each battery had about five miles of line out, and in spite of constant shelling, and tanks churning the line up, it was wonderful how they kept communications through.

During the remainder of October and the beginning of November there was no thought of an attack, it was just a question of holding the line, with the battalions doing constant patrolling. On 1st November a Divisional Club was set up in Geleen, and a percentage of each battery went off every afternoon to the ENSA shows, cinema, cafes and the very excellent showers available at the by-product chemical factory. 129 Battery even ran a dance in the village hall next door to their gun position at Jabeek, which was most successful. The band of the Life Guards came to play, and it was with a certain amount of fear and trepidation that the Colonel allowed it, as he thought that the Leicestershire Yeomanry would never live it down if the position was shelled and the big drum or some other cherished instrument of the band was damaged. There was of course a shortage of girls, being so close to the frontier, and those that came could not speak English, but it was wonderful to see the way the men got on and made themselves understood.

On 1st December General Montgomery, as he then was, made a surprise visit to R.H.Q. at Hillensberg, the Colonel unfortunately was out at the time, but Peter Studd, Bernard Brassey and the remainder at R.H.Q. had great pleasure in introducing him to his first visit on to German soil in the sector. During his visit he told of his plans to start leave back to England in the New Year, which of course was received with very great enthusiasm, the conditions being that everyone would be selected to go by ballot and to have done not less than six months in the theatre.

Later in the day he held an investiture at Divisional H.Q. at which L/Sgt. Ashwell received a well earned M.M. for his very gallant effort during the fighting in Nijmegen.

By this time the Regiment had taken on strength two interpreters! Willie Burki with 130 Battery, who they had got to know in Malden, and had brought down with them, and Jan van Wessen from Sittard, who joined 129 Battery.

And so the days went on. Bernard Brassey had done a great deal of collecting in the way of livestock, and so a regimental farm was set up at Wintraak, which consisted of eight pigs, four goats, three calves and some eighty head of poultry. Prospects for the future were indeed bright!

On the 8th December the dispositions of the regiments changed somewhat, as 7th Armoured Division came into the area, and in consequence the Regiment had to move over slightly, and for the first time it was entirely in Germany, deploying at Gangelt. Everyone was thoroughly sickened by the sight of this small town, for the looting had been absolutely frightful. Nobody minded tables and chairs being removed, or even a door to make a dug-out comfortable, and of course the food stored in the houses was honest booty, but when all the furniture was smashed to pieces, and clothes and broken crockery strewn all over the floor, it was going too far. It was so bad in some cases that the houses earmarked for command posts, etc., had to have a large fatigue party sent on ahead in order to sweep out and burn the contents. Even so, the smell remained, and will never be forgotten by those who were there. O.P.s were established in support of the 1st Welsh Guards at Birgden and Kreuzrath. The former was most unpleasant, and with the forward positions not more than 100 yards from the enemy, it was necessary to keep to the back of the room used as the O.P., as the window was well under observation by the Germans.

On 10th December operation "Shears" was conceived. This was a plan for a united attack up to Heinsberg, and so straighten out the dent which was in the front line. A large amount af ammunition was dumped in preparation, but the weather turned bad, and the country became so boggy that it was impossible to move. The operation was initially postponed, but on the 13th December it was cancelled altogether. However, the ammunition dumped was used in a big counter-battery programme one morning, and it must have made the Germans wonder what was happening or what was going to happen when the terrific concentrations came down after weeks of being limited to eight rounds per gun per day owing to the supply situation. As so often happens, as soon as the operation was finally cancelled, the weather improved.

On 16th December news came through that the Division was going to be pulled out and sent to a rest area near Louvain, the actual move to take place about 24th December. Reconnaissance parties were immediately prepared, and took some organising with the amount of coal, cows and pigs that the batteries wanted to take with them for the Christmas festivities. All the preparations were, however, in vain, as late that evening the plan was changed, and the reconnaissance parties were to go for the day only and return. The reason was the initial success of the German counter-attack in the Ardennes.

On the 19th December reports from the Division's forward troops showed that heavy vehicles were moving about in the enemy lines, and precautions were taken to meet any attack. The move to the rest area was cancelled and the Division was placed on six hours notice to move operationally. The next day all the information pointed to a continual build-up of enemy transport on the Division's front, but afterwards there were strong rumours that they were produced by gramophone records.

On the 20th December the move to the rest area was re-ordered, but it was such short notice that the reconnaissance parties were unable to take all the pigs that they wished. However they set off with a few at 0900 hours, under Bernard Brassey, to the little town of Holsbeek, where they had reconnoitered three days previously. The Division was to move in the afternoon, handing over to the 52nd Division, who were next to it in the line, but very soon it was realised that the German break through the American 1st Army towards the Meuse was much more serious than had at first been supposed. Von Runstedt had collected all his S.S. troops and as much infantry as he could lay his hands on to endeavour to make a decisive break-through with twenty Divisions. The net result was that all the plans were once again changed during the morning, the Division would move, but not to the rest area at Louvain, that further orders would be given at Hasselt, and that almost certainly it would be in an operational role.

There were rumours flying about everywhere, and with plans constantly being changed, no one quite knew what was happening or what to expect. The Regiment finally set off on a very unpleasant journey through the night, the wheels leaving at 1815 hours and the tracks at 2000 hours, and of course a D.R. was sent to Holsbeek to give the reconnaissance party the disappointing news.

CHAPTER FIVE

The Winter

THE move to Hasselt was extremely difficult, with the great quantity of traffic on the roads, and it did not help either having to send the wheels and the tracks on entirely different routes. The Colonel went on ahead with the Signals Officer, Darrell Angus, to try and get some early information, and when they got to Hasselt and the hurriedly established 30th Corps H.Q. there, they found all the Commanding Officers turning up one by one. General Horrocks soon turned up himself, and he asked the General, Brigadier Norman Gwatkin, the C.R.A., George Fanshaw, commanding the Herts. Yeomanry, and the Colonel to go round and have a cup of tea with him. As usual, he was in terrific form and viewed the whole show as a good omen, as he considered it would give the Allies the maximum chance of fighting the whole German Army in the west, this side of the Rhine and the Siegfried Line.

The Colonel and Darrell spent the entire night after this policing the whole Division through Hasselt, and somehow or other by the morning each regiment had arrived intact, and by some miracle or other had managed to sort themselves out.

Orders were that the Division was to be concentrated in area St. Trond-Tirlemont in a counter-attack role, in case of a German penetration across the Meuse. The Regiment was to be deployed in area Halmael-St. Trond to await developments.

Meanwhile Bernard Brassey and his reconnaissance party had rejoined the Regiment, having left what livestock they took down with them at Holsbeek. The batteries had however all brought something with them in their main bodies, 130 Battery even brought five pigs in one S.P.!

The poor Belgians seemed very upset, and quite thought the Germans would soon penetrate back and drive once more to Brussels, but re-assuring news soon came through, for on the 22nd December information was received that the enemy was nowhere nearer than twenty-five miles away, and the Household Cavalry patrolling the banks of the Meuse between Liege and Huy had seen nothing, so the Belgian spirit was revived.

At the same time the Regiment came out of action, and billets were found for everyone. R.H.Q. and 130 Battery stayed in Halmael, and 129 Battery and 131 Battery in the outskirts of St. Trond. Restrictions had to be imposed on personnel going out, as the Regiment was still at four hours notice to move, and the threat of German parachutists was real. Everyone of course was wondering if things would remain calm enough to cover the Christmas period. All preparations went on just the same, and the Quartermaster's staff managed to collect a rare lot of food and fare for the Regiment.

32nd Brigade were most unlucky having to move on Christmas Eve down to the Meuse as a precautionary measure, but they were able to return the next day. They held their Christmas holiday later on in the week. 5th Brigade stayed put, and on Christmas Eve Padre March conducted a splendid carol service which everyone enjoyed, and at which the singing was excellent. That night there was a scare of paratroops on the American airfield close by, and the Regiment had to stand-to in the middle of the night, but it came to nothing.

Christmas Day was spent in the traditional way in the various battery and R.H.Q. areas. They had all found some village hall or barn where everyone could have the meal together, and as usual the cooks did really excellent work.

130 Battery had a concert show in the village hall at Halmael in the evening, which Sam Hughes had started to produce at Gangelt, anticipating a Christmas there. With all the scares and moves, the time for rehearsing was seriously cut down, and taking this into account it was a really first-class show, and much appreciated by all who saw it. Sam Hughes's Choir and the Pantomime-skit of

Cinderella will never be forgotten. The "Battery Show" caught on, and was the first of a series which improved each time, and which started in the remainder of the Regiment as well.

Meanwhile the weather had turned from dull, mild days to very sharp frosts and sunny days, which gave the Air Force the chance they needed so badly to deal with the German advances. These were now becoming somewhat threatening towards Dinant and Givet, to the south of Namur.

On the morning of the 27th December a V-1 flying bomb landed right in the middle of 129 and 131 Battery areas, in fact thirty yards from the latter's Battery Office. It killed a woman and her child, several other civilians were injured, but the Regiment was extremely fortunate in having only three members slightly hurt in 131 Battery, who were soon back from the M.O. proudly displaying their plastered wounds. The bomb did a great deal of damage to the surrounding houses, and the blast must have broken every window for about half a mile all round. It was heard later that at about exactly the same time a V-1 also landed right in the middle of Holsbeek, and just where the regimental billets were going to be, and between the two the Regiment was extremely lucky.

New Year's Day came with the Regiment still under orders to move at short notice, but at six hours instead of four. However, the German threat in the Ardennes was definitely becoming less serious, and the probability of the Division being used in mobile reserve became slight. Therefore it looked as if the stay in the area might be a long one, and accordingly a programme of training for everyone was organised to fill in the days.

At about 0930 hours on New Year's Day the Germans carried out a mass air-raid on all Belgian aerodromes, no doubt hoping to catch everyone in bed, or at any rate with imperial hangovers after the previous night's celebrations, but with the aerodrome next door to the Regimental area at St. Trond they were unlucky. "A" Troop of the 94th L.A.A. were on their toes, and they shot down one Me109, and very severely damaged another, which could not possibly have got back. Considering the few chances they had, "A" Troop's shooting had been magnificent, and since landing in Normandy they claimed twelve "Category 1s" to their credit. Altogether the Germans received a hot reception, for apart from "A" Troop and the aerodrome defences, "D" Troop of 130 Battery were out practising at the time with the .50 Brownings on their tank and S.P.s, and of course they joined in with the terrific amount of flak that was sent up. Altogether three Me.109s were shot down.

On the 5th January a most successful regimental dance was held in St. Trond, and unlike the dance at Nijmegen, this time there was no shortage of girls at all. On the 8th January Captain John Simpson arrived to take over the duties of M.O. in lieu of Lieut. D. M. Colyer.

Meanwhile R.H.Q. continued in rather uncomfortable billets in Halmael, with the officer's mess in a very cramped house belonging to a M. and Mme. Tits, who were not at all easy to get on with. Every time an officer walked in or out through the back entrance all the floors were immediately mopped up. The floors of the kitchens in most of the houses were stone-faced, and could easily have been washed periodically, but no, the mopping and swilling went on everlastingly, with never a thought of a bath for themselves or a good wash for the children.

130 Battery had their mess in the house of M. le Cure, and some of the officers lived in the house of M. and Mme. Celis, who made cognac. They were extremely generous and gave the officers some of the best dinners that they have ever had, but it was felt somehow that they had both been extremely friendly with the Germans in the past. There was great excitement just before the Regiment left the area, when the police came along to search their premises one morning, and found quantities of illicit alcohol in the cellars. M. Celis was taken off to prison, and everything found of course was confiscated. The vast amount of stuff had to be seen to be believed, for apart from the drink there were quantities of bank notes, diamonds, gold watches and coins. He was an extraordinary man, and used to start making his cognac at about nine o'clock every morning with a bucket of what looked like egg powder, and by lunch time he had not only

bottled and labelled cases and cases of this stuff, so called cognac, but sold it as well, mostly to the Americans, and at a very vast profit to himself. Apparently, the charge against him was not for making the stuff for which he had a licence, but for obtaining and using alcohol in the black market for which he had not got a licence! He subsequently served a good many months in prison, but came out early (costing him something in the region of a hundred thousand francs), and his wife was always able to come and give him all the good food obtainable in the black market, and nobody said anything.

129 Battery and 131 Battery had got themselves very comfortable billets in St. Trond, and in all places the population was very friendly, and the men got very well "dug in".

The leave to England started at the beginning of the month, and the Regiment had a very good allotment of vacancies for January. The travelling conditions were shocking though, anything up to eighteen hours in an unheated train from Bourg Leopold to Calais, but definitely regarded by everyone as being well worth it!

Training continued, and included an examination for all technical assistants, officers and men alike, and also some shooting at Lommel, on the Belgian Army artillery ranges, on the 12th, 13th and 14th of January. The former produced some excellent results, and of the twenty-two other-rank specialists who went in for the test, run by the Corps I.G., a high percentage passed out 1st Class, which was very satisfactory. At Lommel there were only two 25-pounders available, both from the 55th Field Regiment, R.A., and so it developed into a ranging competition; very good practice for all the officers, and an excellent opportunity for the Colonel to say in a knowing voice, "You *must* make use of your O.T. rounds!!"

Meanwhile the Russian winter offensive had begun, and Warsaw, Cracow and many other towns fell in a very short time. On the 26th January they were up to the River Oder, and were well inside Germany and menacing Breslau. On the American front in the Ardennes, Von Runstedt's big push of the previous month gradually receded, although the Germans did gain some success in Alsace and towards Strasbourg. On the whole, though, things looked exceedingly bright compared to a month ago.

Training still continued with its many diversions; on the 23rd and 24th January there was some more shooting at Lommel, this time using the Regiment's own guns, taken there on transporters. There were also some tanks of 5th Guards Armoured Brigade firing their guns in conjunction, and this form of indirect fire proved most effective. Apart from this, there were lectures on security, study days for the two Dutch interpreters, tank recognition courses, lectures by the air O.P., instruction in German mines and detonators, exchange visits with the Americans, lectures by an American fighter pilot from the local aerodrome, and many other things.

Leave continued to Brussels, and as the percentage allowed had now increased to $33\frac{1}{3}\%$, short leave parties were also sent to Nijmegen and Eindhoven, and 131 Battery had many requests for a visit to Oss!

The Colonel himself went on leave to England on 28th January, resplendent in a coat with a beautiful white fur collar, which was strongly suspected as having once been the beards of Bernard Brassey's white billy-goats secured in Hillensburg! Bernard himself took over command of the Regiment in the Colonel's absence.

The next day the Divisional Commander visited the Regiment, and on the 31st January Bernard met the Corps Commander. Everything went on quietly in the Regiment, but there was a tension in the air, and everyone knew that something big was bound to be starting soon, and that the winter's rest was coming to an end.

R.H.Q., now moved to St. Trond, had one or two parties in anticipation of a move at the end of the month. Their officers' mess had one on the 30th for a small party of American nurses from a nearby hospital, who were very charming, and the following evening the officers gave another one. This time for *"les jeunes filles de St. Trond,"* and for all friends of Mme. Velaers, in whose house they were, and both parties were very successful.

On the 31st January orders came through for the next battle, to be known as operation "Veritable," and as a result the guns and tanks had to leave next morning on their journey to Nijmegen. All the orders were very secret, and no one knew when the push was going to start. When they got there, with all the G.P.O.s, they were shown their gun positions by the C.R.A. These were in the woods S.E. of Nijmegen, very close to the old regimental positions, and a part of the world that few, if any, of the Regiment had ever hoped to see again. The guns arrived after dark on the 2nd February, and by morning were well and truly hidden, should there have been any prying eyes of the German Air Force. It seemed strange to be motoring back over old battlefields, with everything much the same as four months previously, the burnt-out tanks, the up-ended 88-mm. guns, all still in the same positions, the only difference being the roads, which in most cases had become quite apalling.

Meanwhile all the wheeled vehicles and the remainder of the Regiment remained back in the St. Trond area. On the 3rd February, 130 Battery gave another edition of their battery concert, or "Sam Hughes' Follies" as it came to be called, and it far surpassed the first edition. It was unfortunate that the whole battery could not be present, but the village hall was absolutely packed to capacity with all the civilian population that could get in.

The remainder of the Regiment finally moved on the 6th February. The destination was only given out to the officers the day before, and all signs on vehicles were completely blacked-out, so hush-hush was the move. Everyone was sorry to leave, as a great number of friends had been made in the area, but at the same time it was felt that the war would never be won by staying there, and it was a very good thing to be going back into action and having another crack at the enemy. Everyone was given a great send-off, all the population turned out, especially the girls, and many a tear was shed.

CHAPTER SIX

From the Reichswald Forest to the Rhine

THE route from St. Trond was through Tilburg, s'Hertogenbosch, Oss and then Nijmegen. The Regiment left St. Trond at 1400 hours, 6th February, but came to a halt at 3 o'clock the following morning at Oss, where there was the most appalling traffic jam imaginable. A lot of vehicles in front had driven off the road, and this was blocked for miles. It was four-and-a-half hours before the move resumed, and Nijmegen was not reached until 0900 hours. The Division meanwhile was staying back in the area of Tilburg, as it was only the artillery that was wanted for the first phase of the battle.

The G.P.O.s were immediately presented with a vast fire-plan for the operation, which was to start at 0500 hours the next day, and included a three-hour smoke-screen and three long lists of concentrations. The guns came out of their hides during the afternoon, and the gunners were kept very busy preparing the ammunition that had been dumped and which came to 600 rounds per gun.

After the initial bombardment on the 8th, the main attack of operation "Veritable" started to go in at 1030 hours with a three-divisional front (51st Highland, 53rd Welsh and 15th Scottish), with 43rd Division following up. There were also a mass of flame-throwers, flails and other jolly little inventions to assist these divisions. Bob Rowland Clark went to H.Q. 53rd Division to act as liaison officer for the smoke screen which was to enable that division to cross the open from Groesbeek up to the western edge of the Reichswald Forest. The screen was very successful, and he returned at the conclusion of it. 130 Battery had to fire red smoke on to Kranenburg, as an indication for the R.A.F. to bomb it, but unfortunately the clouds were very low, although the planes were heard arriving, as usual, dead on time. As far as the Regiment was concerned, this finished its part in the British Army fire-plan. The noise in the gun area was terrific, as there were upward of a thousand guns in a comparatively small space, ranging from 25-pounders to super-heavies and "Long Toms."

The Regiment however had still to support the Canadians, who were not starting their attack until 1800 hours. Concentrations were fired in support of them for about three-quarters-of-an-hour. Their plan was to clean up the country between the Rhine and the Nijmegen-Kranenburg-Cleve road. A very great part of this was under water, and they had to go into battle using "Buffaloes" and "Ducks." However, despite this, they got on remarkably quickly.

Early reports which came in of the attack showed that things were going well. Many German guns had been knocked out in the bombardment, endless Germans had been killed, and hundreds and hundreds of prisoners taken, and a lot of them so "bomb-happy" that they were only too willing to give themselves up.

During the night the attack continued, aided by hundreds of searchlights directed towards the enemy, or "artificial moonlight" as it was called. Another concentration was fired at 0120 hours, and a further one at 0840 hours. The Regiment remained on call all through the 9th February, but by 1400 hours it was out of range of the front line except for two small areas which could be engaged with supercharge only. That night all the gunners had a very good and well earned sleep, and the next day was spent in maintaining the guns and cleaning up the ammunition salvage.

The weather was now very bad, and indeed could not have been worse for the operation. A period of really soaking rain set in, and the floods gradually grew larger and deeper, making more remote the prospect of the Guards Armoured Division being loosed into the battle. And so the Regiment sat day after day in the rain, in the same gun positions, whilst the infantry divisions slogged and sloshed their way forward.

The Colonel returned to the Regiment on the 9th

February, to be greeted that evening by an air-raid. A rare amount of "ack-ack" greeted the raiders, but the Colonel showed little enthusiasm for the beautiful display of pyrotechnics, it was suspected that his mind was far away with the Atherstone hounds which he had just left, having had three days' hunting and a day's racing at Cheltenham during a magnificent week's leave.

The Regiment stayed put between the 10th and 22nd February. Where possible, billets were found for the men, but this was not easy with the tremendous number of administrative troops in the area for the big battle. During the period advantage was taken of ENSA and baths, etc., in Nijmegen, but apart from that it was maintenance and rest in preparation for what was obviously coming. The rest of the Division moved up from Tilburg, and the infantry battalions went into the battle about the 16th February; it was still too early to use the armour.

On the 10th it was reported that Cleve had fallen, and on the 12th Gennep. By the 13th the Reichswald had been cleared by the 53rd Division. It was a lovely forest, or rather had been before the barrage, but when visited by the Colonel and Bob Hoare on the morning of the 14th, there was hardly a tree which was unmarked by shell-fire. They saw some 12.2-cm. guns in a German battery position which had been knocked out, and in the various dug-outs used as Command Posts there were many German dead, and one still lying in his bunk. On the way back they saw Field-Marshal Montgomery returning from the Canadian sector in a "Duck."

On the 16th Asperden was taken by the 52nd Division, and Goch fell to the 15th Scottish Division on the 19th.

At last, on the evening of the 22nd February, orders came through to go into action. The plan was for 5th Brigade and the Regiment in support to take over a part of the line north of Goch. The wheels and tracks left separately the next day, and both parties had the most appalling journey down to the area. There was only the one main road down, and this was just one long line of vehicles nose-to-tail going in both directions. To relieve the congestion there was even a railway being built beside the road, and, having done the same trip two or three times it was

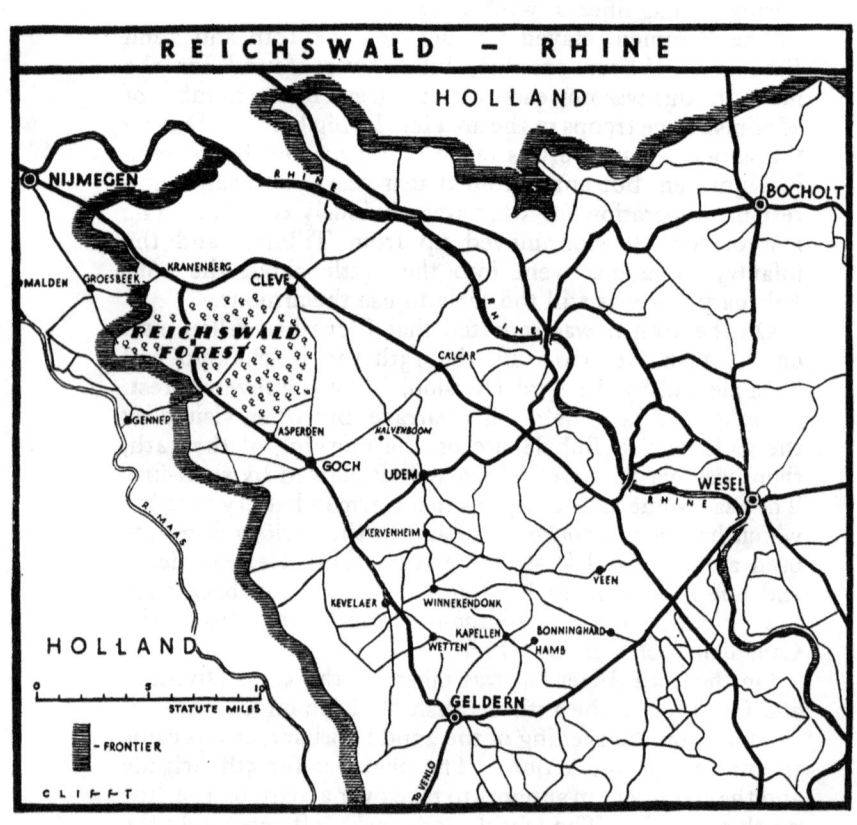

Crossing the Rhine

Sandbostel Prison Camp

Wrecked Sherman Firefly

astonishing to see how quickly it was constructed. The whole countryside was in the most awful chaotic state as a result of the battle, every house and tree was smashed, and German equipment and debris lay about everywhere.

By the evening of the 23rd the Regiment was in action, and there was one O.P. supporting the Grenadiers, which was Jerry Green at Holvenboom. It was a most unpleasant spot, the village was completely devastated, and all the approaches were in view and drew heavy fire. During the three days he was there, the O.P. had several direct hits, but he and his crew were fortunate and had no casualties.

Very soon there was a mass of ammunition dumped by the guns, in order to support the Canadians who were going to attack the next day between Uden and Calcar. There were endless shoots done, both observed and predicted, and on the 26th, when the attack started at 0300 hours, the Regiment hardly stopped firing the whole day. One of the infantry regiments, the Regiment de Chaumeire, had their start-line in the leading company area of the Grenadiers, and Bob Hoare arranged for a squadron of tanks to give covering fire in the initial stage, which proved to be very successful.

On the 27th Uden was taken, and on the 28th Kervenheim, on both of which large concentrations were fired by the Regiment before the attack went in.

For some time now the enemy had been very greatly reinforced, as was anticipated and planned by the Allied staffs, so that when the Americans broke out from the Aachen sector they would be able to reach the Rhine comparatively easily. Two Panzer divisions were now in action, 6th Para. Division, and certain other infantry divisions as well.

A very high rate of fire was kept up by the guns until 1st March, when the Regiment became out of range. Reconnaissance parties were sent forward to prepare to take over positions occupied by 3rd Division as soon as Kervenheim was taken. The Regiment expected to move immediately, but owing to stiff opposition the move was delayed. The next day it did move forward, but no sooner had the position been reached than it was ordered to return again, as the Corps Commander considered that the time was ripe to launch the Division as a whole.

The Regiment had orders to move at midnight, but actually did not move until midnight the following night, the 3rd. Times were altered, and plans were changed, and the number of times that vehicles were loaded and unloaded and "bivvies" put up and down was quite extraordinary.

The Division's objective was Bonninghardt, and the route down was through Kevelaer and Kapellen, but this was altered several times as various bridges were found blown and roads cratered, and it was found impossible to get at the latter place, having arrived at Wetton at first light after a very cold and wet night. The roads were quite unbelievable, and had virtually disappeared after the heavy rain. It seemed a miracle how the supplies and the mass of ammunition which was fired ever got up.

On the 4th the Irish Group led, with the Regiment going into action east of Winnekendonk to support the Group into Hamb. This was overlooked from the woods and high ground to the north, and Chris Vesey and Jack Howard with their crews had a very unpleasant thirty-six hours before these were cleared.

Meanwhile the Grenadiers, who had been trying to push on from Wetton but were held up by craters, retraced their steps, and on the afternoon of the 5th put in an attack to clear the remainder of the woods N.W. of Hamb, towards Bonninghardt. The Regiment fired two programmes in support of this, which the Colonel and Bob Hoare conceived, and which proved very satisfactory. Afterwards it was seen that, apart from every tree which was smashed to pieces, there were two enemy guns knocked out, and a large quantity of ammunition "brewed up." There were also several very successful regimental opportunity targets done by Jerry Green, and the Group reached its objective with very few casualties.

Meanwhile the Americans had for several days now been driving northwards to Venlo and beyond, and it was on the 3rd that the link-up took place between them and the 8th Armoured Brigade in Geldern. The whole of the German defence was altered at once, and his great object was to hold a bridgehead south-west of Wesel for as long as possible, to get back as many troops and as much equipment as possible. There was no doubt that the parachute divisions were fighting extremely hard and well, and were a vastly tougher nut to crack than the ordinary infantry.

On the 6th the Regiment moved up into action in the wooded area just captured, and the Grenadiers were ordered forward again, to hold a part of the line south-east of Veen. Jerry Green had the worst O.P. that the battery ever had to occupy, and he was shelled and mortared for a complete day and night. However, no harm was done, and the Regiment fired a tremendous number of rounds at the ever decreasing German bridgehead.

By the 9th it was all over, and there followed two peaceful days in the Regimental area resting and maintaining. It was interesting to work out the colossal ammunition expenditure, for it was found that since the commencement of operation "Veritable" to the collapse of the Wesel bridgehead, the Regiment fired approximately 3,000 rounds per gun, more than during the whole of the rest of the campaign.

It was in this area that Sidney Hedges returned to the Regiment, looking very hale and hearty, having recovered from his wound received at St. Martin des Besages.

On the 12th March the Regiment was ordered back to Nijmegen to rest and refit and once again prepare for the next operation. The whole Division moved back into that area, and for once there was the most wonderful weather. The time was fully occupied changing tracks, re-fitting bogeys, stripping guns, and doing all the hundred and one things that always have to be done. Apart from this there were the usual football matches, hockey matches against the Quick Club, and short leave started again. Unofficial leave parties were also sent by special request to St. Trond and Halmael, where they were given the most wonderful welcome, to say nothing of the gifts of eggs, etc., for themselves, and for the others who were not fortunate enough to go.

Everyone was in excellent billets on the edge of the town, and, as before, the people were extremely kind. Just outside at Malden, the progress of the new airfield being constructed was watched with great interest. It was built at an amazing speed, and by the morning of the 21st it was full of Tempests and Typhoons.

On the 14th March the splendid announcement was made that the Colonel had been awarded the D.S.O. He attributed it entirely to the exceptionally good work of everyone in the Regiment, but the Regiment definitely thought otherwise.

On the 21st March he attended a very large conference at 30th Corps H.Q. at Pfalzdorf, in which General Horrocks gave a very full and interesting account of the plans he had worked out for crossing the Rhine. Meanwhile the Colonel and Bernard had been down on several occasions to reconnoitre the gun positions in the area opposite Rees, and it was quite obvious that hiding and camouflage were going to be a serious problem as the area was very far forward and open. Every precaution was to be taken, and for days beforehand enormous smoke screens, sixty miles long, were created along the banks of the Rhine, and inland too, so that aerial observation could not see the traffic on the main roads in the area, and to keep the Germans guessing.

Sidney Hedges had by this time taken over command of "C" Troop, as Derek Baer was taken ill with jaundice on his way back from leave in England.

On the afternoon of 22nd March, the reconnaissance parties set off through the Reichswald and the ruins of Calcar to a little village called Gesthuysen, which was the regimental deployment area.

The guns left Nijmegen in the evening, and the move went without a hitch, arriving fifteen minutes early for a change, just after midnight. The advance parties had previously suffered a most unpleasant four or five hours when the wind suddenly changed and the smoke screen, instead of blowing away blew into their faces. It was slightly toxic and made everyone realise the horror of gas. The Colonel and Bernard coughed their insides out, and subsided—supper being out of the question. It was a great relief when it was decided to call the screen off, as four men in the R.H.Q. building had already been evacuated!

Only the guns, command posts, and other essential

vehicles came down into the area, as with the vast numbers of troops and vehicles that would shortly be in the area before the assault across the river, it was necessary to cut down to a bare minimum. The administrative vehicles and the remainder of the Regiment therefore all went into harbour in the Reichswald Forest.

Great quantities of ammunition had been dumped by parties the Regiment had sent about four nights before, all carefully camouflaged, and when the guns arrived they all went into barns and buildings, all very carefully planned out beforehand, so that when daylight came there was nothing to be seen at all, the weather was perfect and the country looked wonderfully peaceful, without any signs of military activity.

At twelve o'clock on the 23rd the area suddenly became full of activity, as it was the time for the guns to go into action. From then on there was no rest for the gunners or the command post staffs. 400 rounds per gun had to be moved from their hides, and vast fire-plans had to be worked out, quite apart from the usual slit trenches to be dug, which seemed very important here as the area seemed terribly vulnerable to shelling, and all by five o'clock, when the firing on operation "Plunder," as it was called, was due to begin.

At five o'clock it did in fact start, and the Regiment never let up until about ten o'clock the next morning. The assault was being made in support of the 51st Highland Division, and all the approaches to the river had been very carefully marked out with white tape and went straight through the regimental position. All through the night there were boats and wheeled vehicles moving up one track, "Buffaloes" and tanks moved up on another, and on the third came the infantry of the Highland Division with their pipes playing, a truly wonderful sight. The organisation seemed absolutely perfect, and good news of progress kept coming in to the Regiment. By half-past nine that night a battalion of the Argyll and Sutherland Highlanders and one from the Black Watch were all across, and by midnight the Gordons as well.

At ten o'clock the next morning, a wonderful spring one, it was known that the 6th British Airborne Division and the 17th U.S.A. Airborne were due to arrive. Sure enough, at eight minutes to the hour, the wonderful sight of the first waves of Dakotas came into view. At a low altitude, and in perfect formation, the first waves passed over, and then a few minutes after ten, they returned empty on their homeward journey. After this there was wave after wave in continual procession, later on with the small gliders, and then the big ones towed by the four-engined Halifaxes.

Casualties appeared to be amazingly light; of all the planes that went over, one Dakota was seen returning with a large chunk out of its wing, and a Stirling bomber crashed within a mile of the regimental position.

So the build-up went on, the bridges over the river were begun, and altogether in forty-eight hours the Regiment fired something in the nature of 1,200 rounds per gun.

On the 26th March the Regiment moved up close to the river to get a little extra range, and the Colonel and many others walked down to look across the river. The bridges were getting on well, and Rees could be seen the other side, absolutely flat and still smouldering.

There was a thunderstorm that evening, and, whilst it was on, the Germans sent over some airburst shells, but fortunately not near enough to be unpleasant, although Sgt. Harrison in 130 Battery had a bit which bounced off his shoulder! It was quite extraordianary that all the time during the Reichswald battle, and the Rhine crossing, with all the thousands of shells that the Regiment sent over, there was never anything sent back at the Regiment by the Germans.

When it was out of range the Regiment settled down where it was, joined by this time with all the echelon vehicles and personnel from the Reichswald. R.H.Q. was in the garden and orchard of a small country pub, with 130 Battery close to it, and 129 and 131 Battery forward near the flood bank and just short of the Rhine. Even though the Regiment was not firing, there were still medium and heavy guns firing, and at times the noise was terrific. It rather upset Bernard's bantam cock which he acquired from the last farm, a really beautiful bird, but the hens didn't seem to worry a bit.

General Allan Adair came round to see the Regiment here, and seemed very pleased with all that had been done, and looked forward to what Monty called "cracking about the plains of northern Germany and the last round."

On the 29th March orders came through for the Division to cross, and on the 30th it did so in complete darkness. The orders were very interesting, giving a centre line which ended up with Bremen and Hamburg! The plan was to push on N.N.E. and through the bridgehead as rapidly as possible, passing through the 3rd British Division, which it did by first light on the 30th.

CHAPTER SEVEN

East of the Rhine

THE Grenadiers led the field, closely followed by 130 Battery as usual, then Brigade H.Q. and the rest of the Regiment. Behind came the Irish Group and then Divisional H.Q. and 32nd Brigade. The route led into Isselburg, where bridges had been built overnight over the Issel. Then right-handed, leaving Anholt on the left where fighting was still proceeding, and on through Dinxperlo.

The Grenadier Group however found it very difficult to get on, as it was constantly coming up against trouble in the shape of road blocks, mines and craters, which were the bugbear throughout the whole of operation "Plunder." The road blocks consisted of felled trees, and as there were always mines laid in the same area, they always took some time to remove.

The Irish Group tried to find another way to the left, and the Regiment, less 130 Battery, followed them, and by nightfall was deployed south of Aalten. From here onwards the fighting was extremely difficult and not very fast, although sometimes the Regiment travelled eighteen or twenty miles in a day. The difficulties were firstly the craters, etc., secondly the very bad, wet going, and lastly the odd 88-mm. or self-propelled gun well-sited in a corner of a wood with a few crazy paratroops, who fought hard and often "brewed-up" the leading two or three vehicles. These bandit parties often had unlimited supplies of "basookas" or Panzerfausts, which did the Sherman tanks just no good at all.

Aalten was lightly held by the enemy, and the Regiment fired red smoke on a large water-tower suspected as an enemy O.P., as an indicator for the Typhoons. Everyone could see them come in, it must have been terrifying for the Germans, and they scored four direct hits on the tower with their rockets. This form of attack became very popular, as it was undoubtedly extremely successful, and worked well with the R.A.F., and from then on there were always large stocks of red smoke kept in the batteries, and a great deal of it was used.

On the 31st March the Regiment went on through Aalten and Lightenvoorde to Groenlo. All the time a good number of prisoners were being taken. It was pleasant to be back in Holland again, and to know and see how pleased the people were. It brought back memories of Brussels, Eindhoven and last September as a whole. The Regiment fired as little as was absolutely necessary on to any of the villages and towns.

Groenlo looked as though it would be a difficult nut to crack, as it had a moat all round the town, but a route was found to the right and the town was by-passed. The air O.P. reported large numbers of enemy withdrawing to the north of the town, and so the Regiment went into action and did some good shoots on these.

The Grenadiers then pushed on to Eibergen, where there was some more light opposition, just as it was getting dark. However there was no rest, as they were ordered to capture the town during the night, so that the Irish could pass through in the morning. This was carried out very well, and the Regiment supported the attack, plus a troop of medium guns from the 84th Medium Regiment, R.A. They always stayed with the Regiment's guns, a new idea, deploying at the same time, and being an advance reconnaissance party, so-to-speak, to their own regiment following up some way behind, should the situation become serious or static enough for them to be called in.

The troop did extremely good work, and it was very useful having something heavier than a 25-pounder immediately available.

On 1st April the Irish went through as planned, and the good work went on through Haaksbergen and on up to the outskirts of Enschede, where a great misfortune befell the Regiment. Willie Burki in his captured Opel van, went off by himself to visit his grandmother at Hengelo, thinking the road between the two towns was clear, and half-way between the two was taken prisoner in an ambush, the same one that also captured the Chief Signals Officer at 30th Corps H.Q.

At Enschede again there were the usual road-blocks and craters, but again another route was found round to the right, over a very bad road, and on the morning of the 2nd Oldenzaal was passed, then right-handed and once more over the border into Germany. The whole countryside round here was completely dominated by a castle at Bentheim, and, with the Irish leading, the advance was held up just short of it in a village called Gildehaus. The Regiment went into action here after witnessing the Typhoons play havoc with the whole place, and it was well on fire when the guns moved in.

All day on the 3rd was taken in plastering Bentheim, the Grenadiers passed through the Irish, and were being very wary, for no sooner had they done so than their first three tanks were "brewed up." However, the subsequent shooting seemed very effective, and later on some knocked-out guns were seen. It was not until the evening that the town was captured, but there were a lot of prisoners taken.

The 4th was spent consolidating, and mopping up in the area, including some good red wine from the Town Hall! Brigadier Norman, the Colonel and many other officers went up to the top of the castle tower, from which there was a really wonderful view. It was hoped to see the 53rd Division advancing from the south, but there was no sign of them. Instead a calibration shoot was carried out! Brigade H.Q. was situated actually at the customs-house just on the border, and it was amazing to notice how, now that the Germans had left, all the Dutch folk with their horses and carts or hand-carts, were having a real good loot! Perhaps loot is not quite the right word, as the Germans had had so many of their belongings, just getting their own back a little!

An amusing incident happened on the 5th, when a squadron company group of the Grenadiers, with Sidney Hedges supporting them, was given the job of clearing Schuttorf to the east, which had been "Typhooned" the day before. As they got into the town, the leading troop-leader saw a gun protruding round a corner, so he withdrew his troop, and Sidney brought down a good concentration on to it. When they advanced they found it was an old brass gun with a cannon-ball lying beside it!

April 6th was spent resting, but on the 7th the advance continued again, up north to join 32nd Brigade, who had for some time taken another centre line, and had been battling for the crossings over the River Ems, and the Dortmund-Ems canal at Lingen. They had formed a bridgehead on the other side, and everyone hoped that 5th Brigade would be able to go right through and have a clear run to Bremen. The Irish led, but very soon were met by more opposition than was expected. The Regiment deployed at once between Lingen and Furstenau, and came in for a fair amount of shelling, especially 129 Battery who were furthest forward. The flash from their guns could obviously be seen by the Germans, and they were extremely fortunate that they suffered only two casualties. All the batteries moved further back, and eventually spent the night there.

Most of the Regiment came in for something that afternoon, the Colonel and Bernard as well. The former was all right with his tank, but not so the latter, who was bracketted plus and minus, but fortunately got away with it.

On the 8th the Irish captured Furstenau, and on the 9th the Grenadiers took the lead. The fighting was extremely difficult in the very wooded country, and all three squadron company groups were committed. The Regiment was in action for the whole time, and eventually Bippen was reached by dark, with a good bag of prisoners taken for the day, including ten men and one officer who gave themselves up in a position of 130 Battery. It was at least half-an-hour after the guns had moved in when they suddenly appeared, armed to the teeth, from a very cleverly constructed and well concealed defensive position within thirty yards of the echelon vehicles!

On the 10th the area round Kettenkamp had to be cleared, and it took most of the day to clear the wood around it. This was done by the Grenadiers, who were particularly pleased with the Regiment's support, for they said that they were able to stand up and watch the shells fall and kill the Germans on the edge of the wood only about 300 yards in front of them.

After a much needed day's rest on the 11th, the advance continued on the 12th. The Irish led once more, and once more the same opposition was met. They captured Cappeln, and by the 14th the Regiment was in the area of Buhren. The Grenadiers the previous evening had had a most successful shoot when their leading tanks caught up with a column of German transport retreating, and they shot up three horse-drawn ammunition waggons, two 75-mm. guns and two lorries. The road was so blocked that they could not move any further that night.

On the evening of the 14th, the Division was ordered to concentrate near Buhren, where it was to be in Corps reserve with the prospect of a three days rest. The Regiment concentrated in a very pleasant area, and at once all the necessary arrangements were made to bath and get in good order again.

After two days it was said that there would be at least another four before a move took place, but before the evening was out orders arrived for a move the next day! The Division was to be transferred to 12th Corps, and was to be used to mop up the country between Bremen and Hamburg. It meant leaving the much liked 30th Corps, and its gallant commander, General Horrocks, and moving round by a south-easterly route to cross the Weser, a journey of some seventy miles.

The advance parties went on ahead, and eventually came to rest at Lichtenmoor, a little village N.E. of Nienburg. The journey for the Regiment was like many others; instead of crossing the start-point at twelve o'clock, they did not get going till nearly three, because of the shocking traffic hold-ups, and did not arrive until the early hours of the morning, after a really shocking journey. All the country that it passed through was lovely. Most of the roads were lined with apple trees, and all the fields looked very green and lovely with a background of pine trees. There was hardly any damage to be seen, and the villages were very picturesque, being mostly of red-brick half-timbered houses.

Whilst waiting for the Regiment to arrive, the Colonel and Bernard Brassey, with the three battery captains, Peter Winslow, Donald Salt and Leslie Yates, witnessed the most extraordinary thunderstorm. It happened at about a quarter-to-nine in the evening, and after it had passed away, the colours of the red-roofed cottages and the green corn fields had to be seen to be believed, they were just like some exotic futuristic painting.

The Regiment had to advance the next day, and the ultimate object was to cut the autobahn between Bremen and Hamburg. 32nd Brigade was already in action, but 5th Brigade pushed on and beyond them to their right. *En route* a magnificent sight was passed at Retham, two completely burnt-out flak trains, each consisting of four "ack-ack" guns. Some were 88-mms., but other were much bigger, and it looked as if they had been well and truly dealt with by the Typhoons.

The plan was that the Brigade should follow up behind the 7th Armoured Division, which had got on very well, as far as Tostedt, and then to swing west, cutting the autobahn and capturing Zeven.

On the way the Regiment had its first view of released British prisoners of war, and a wonderful sight it was. Lorry after lorry load of them passed by, all cheering wildly, having just been released from the nearby camp at Filingbostel.

Before turning left a night was spent on the way, and on the 19th the Grenadiers set off in the lead. The autobahn was soon cut, and very little opposition was met, and for that night the Regiment went into action near Weirtzen. During the night two German aeroplanes strafed the harbour area of the Grenadiers, and Dick Bentley, who was working with them, had a lucky escape. He was sleeping in the usual hole in the ground with a two-man tent over him, when a bullet went through his hair! In the morning he saw eleven holes in the tent!

The next day the Grenadiers made some of the approaches to Zeven, and captured a couple of villages, but fighting was not a bit easy, and the opposition had considerably stiffened. The Regiment remained where it was, and fired a good many rounds in support.

The Irish Group were now given the job of clearing the villages of Elsdorf, Wistedt and Frankenbostel. These proved to be very hotly contested battles, and during the 21st and 22nd April Chris Vesey, Jack Howard and Mike Townsend all had very unpleasant spells, especially at the village of Elsdorf, which was bombed and shelled heavily, and also counter-attacked in the middle of the night. Mike Townsend indeed had to descend by the belfry rope after the church which he was using as an O.P. had received a direct hit, and the ladders blown away. Needless to say, Mike, who was always ready for the fray, was soon up it again. It was extremely dangerous, but he was not deterred, and it was only by ordering the R.E.s to blow it up that the commander of the Irish Group could prevent him from using it again. The commander, incidentally, was extremely pleased with the support that had been given him in what was obviously a ticklish situation, and after this battle was over he personally spoke to all 129 Battery and thanked them for what they had done. Most of the enemy encountered were the 15th Panzer Grenadiers, and had evidently been ordered to keep the road from Bremen to the north open, as the autobahn had been cut.

On the 23rd April, the Grenadiers and Coldstreams were given the task of clearing Zeven. As a preliminary to the attack the Regiment was to fire red smoke on the town for some Mitchell bombers. When they eventually arrived, one load of bombs came down on the target, but one load definitely did not, and landed only about 800 yards from the regimental position. The main attack went in on the 24th, and, with the Regiment firing many concentrations, the town was taken without much difficulty, but, once inside, the Group had a most unpleasant time, being shelled incessantly. The Regiment moved up, and went into action on the outskirts of the town, and 131 Battery reconnaissance party were unfortunate to have three casualties by being caught in this shelling. Later on, patrols from 130 and 131 Batteries were met by a hail of Spandau fire soon after leaving the position. It was obvious that the enemy were extremely close to the north, so the Regiment moved back again for the night.

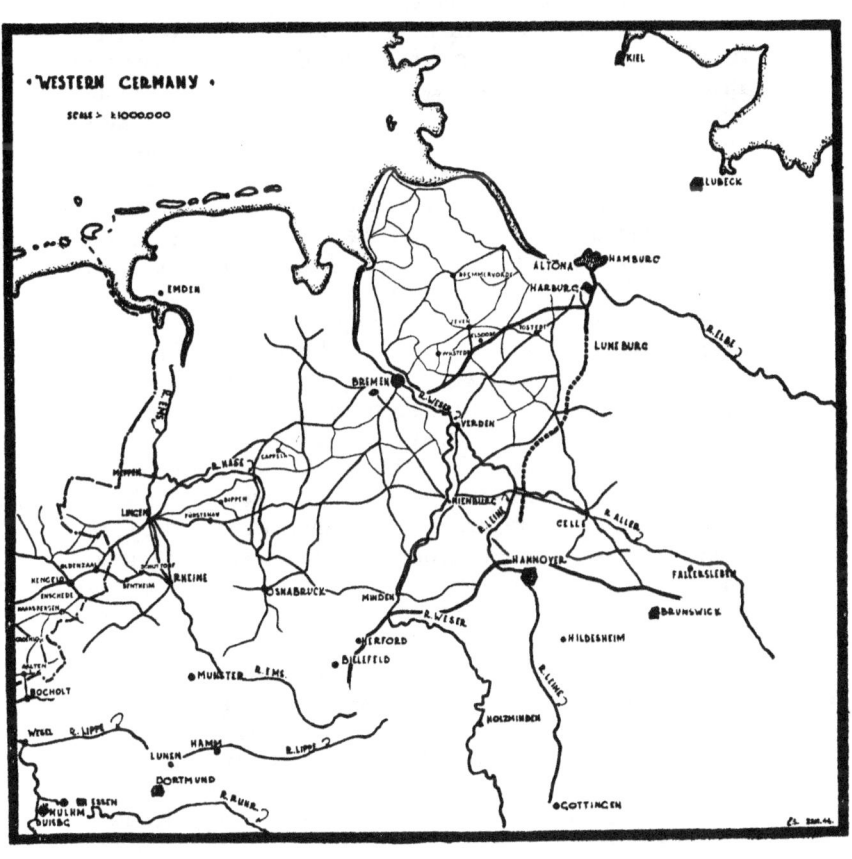

During this time John Patterson had been acting Adjutant in the place of Peter Studd, who was on leave in England. Nobody had ever been seen to look forward to his leave so much as Peter!

For this action, Brigade H.Q. was in the village of Weertzen. It was a very happy party, with Tom Blackwell as Brigade Major, Angus Hardy doing D.A.A.Q.M.G., and Father Lack always in good form. It was during this time that, returning from one of his many visits to Brussels, Father Lack was halted, probably for lunch, when he was attacked by a bull. That part of the story was probably true, but the outcome of it was that the bull, having chased Father Lack first into a latrine, then round a tree, fell a victim to the rifle shot of a Guardsman! At all events, the next night the mess had a sirloin of extremely good beef for dinner, so Father Lack must have had the situation well in hand and quickly called for a butcher. The mess was feeding extremely well, and next night there was a goose for dinner. Again Father Lack was asked from where it came, and his reply was that the poor thing succumbed to the *ricochet* of the bullet that killed the bull—wicked old man!

O.P.s were established on the far side of Zeven, and an especially good one in the church of the town itself. When the Grenadiers were firmly established in that area, the Regiment was ordered through the town and into action on the far side. The plan was for 32nd Brigade to pass through, and continue the advance to the west, and the Regiment would be available to give any additional support that was necessary. It was whilst reconnoitering this position that Bernard driving a jeep himself, set off a mine down a narrow lane. The two front wheels and the whole of the front part of the jeep went up, and he and Sgt. Knowles, who was with him, were extremely fortunate in getting away with only light injuries. Sgt. Knowles sprained a leg, and Bernard, as it eventually transpired, broke a small bone in his foot. There is no doubt that the advice learnt in Normandy of having sandbags on the floor of every vehicle must have very largely saved them. Even "Belinda" and the other bantams carried at the back of the jeep were untouched, but of course escaped! After

Part of R.H.Q. near Achim

V.E. Sunday, Cadenberge Forest

Ready for G.O.C.'s Inspection

two days at "A" echelon when his foot didn't seem to be getting any better, Bernard unfortunately had to be evacuated, and Bob Rowland Clark took over as second-in-command.

After this, the Regiment moved into the area, everyone keeping a sharp look-out for more mines, and good many more were found. 130 Battery came in for a certain amount of shelling from a S.P. gun, and rounds fell right amongst the guns and vehicles; luckily no damage or casualties were caused.

On the 28th, 32nd Brigade were going to be left whilst 5th Brigade was to move north towards Bevern, with the Grenadiers leading. The Regiment moved up to Selsingen and went into action, and very soon Bevern was captured. The General and Brigadier Norman then came up, and a plan was made to liberate Sandbostel Prison Camp, which was originally going to be the task for the infantry next day.

Bob Hoare was on leave, so Peter Winslow had taken over 130 Battery and joined the Grenadiers. Things did not go as easily as expected, and the one Squadron Company Group which was given the task had to be reinforced by the whole of the rest of the Group before the place could be cleared, which was eventually done on the 30th.

The military part of the camp was not too terrible, but there were also about 4,000 civilians, anti-Nazis and Jews, and these were so starved and stricken that there were heaps of dead corpses lying about the place. There were hundreds and hundreds of them mad with disease and hunger who were quite unable to move. The guards of the camp were all S.S. men, and it appeared that the whole place was just as bad as anything found at Belsen and many others, only perhaps on a smaller scale.

Meanwhile, whilst this was going on, the Irish had pushed on past Bevern, and tried to get to Bremervorde, but the bridge was blown on the way to the town.

On 1st May came the news that the Division would move to the N.E., and would probably have a 36-hour rest. The regimental area was Essel. Whilst waiting in Bevern to join in the column which was going through, a heavy gun began to shell the village, and 131 Battery were unfortunately caught. One shell landed between G.E.

half-track and Sgt. Clampit's S.P. Three men were killed and three wounded, including Randall of Leicester (killed) and Bdr. Core of Melton Mowbray (wounded). Everyone was most upset about this, especially as the war was obviously in its closing stages, for the wireless was continually giving out news of whole German divisions surrendering, etc.

The 36-hour rest came to nothing, as the Regiment, soon after it arrived at Essel, received orders to go into action first thing in the morning to support the Irish who were to clear the area to the north, and later on, as they advanced, the Regiment moved to Hagenham.

Somehow there was an air of great expectancy, and the feeling that the Germans had had enough was prevalent. The news of the surender on the Italian front had come through, and it was noticed that it was signed on a Sunday, although not actually taking effect until the Wednesday, and it was felt throughout the Regiment that the same thing was happening on the 2nd Army Front.

On the 3rd came the fall of Berlin, and Hamburg declared an open city, together with the surrender of German troops in Denmark. It was on this day that Jack Howard fired the Regiment's last target: "Mike Target, Mike Target, Mike Target, M.4 Map reference 974546, Height 11 metres, Description of target, Village in enemy hands."

At 1820 hours on 5th May the great news came through that all the Germans on the 2nd Army front had surrendered. Although this did not mean the end of the war for everyone, it looked a good bet as far as the Regiment was concerned, so what drink there was available was produced, and at any rate in R.H.Q. everyone had a good tot of whisky.

On 6th May the Regiment fired a Victory Salvo of flares at 0750, as the formal surrender was taking effect as from 0800 hours. The flares were all different coloured shells which had been carried by the S.P.s all through the campaign and never used, and those were the last rounds fired.

After this, the Colonel, with Vokins and Eric Sowman went up to Hamburg, rather hoping to pick up a nice civilian car. Unfortunately they were a bit too late, but it was extremely interesting to see the condition of the place, which must have been a lovely town before the R.A.F. got at it. No remorse could be felt looking at the huge heaps of rubble, the Boche had asked for it and got it. Yet there were smartly turned-out women walking about, and shoals of Germans coming in, not quite knowing what to do or where to go. It was incredible to think where all the civilians lived, it appeared that the majority existed in cellars.

On 7th May preparations were made to take over the area held by the enemy in the area of Cuxhaven, where the whole of the Division's bitter enemy, 7th Parachute Division, was to be assembled by this time.

The Brigadier held a conference in which he said, "No more corduroys, no more neckerchiefs, no more private cars, just vigorous discipline and soldiering. We have to teach these Boches and go on teaching them until they get tired of fighting. But they never will, after ten months of fighting, they will never alter, it's bred in them too deeply. My God! What an unattractive race they are, but they are efficient."

Soon after the conference was over, came the wonderful news that peace had been declared, and that the Germans had accepted unconditional surrender on all fronts to the Allies. In the evening Mr. Churchill made a short, stirring speech, mainly reminding everyone of their duty in the future, and proclaimed the morrow as VE-Day.

On 13th May, VE-Sunday, Padre March, who had been with the Regiment quite a while (ever since poor Padre Pryor was killed in Normandy), conducted a General Thanksgiving Service. As many as possible of the Regiment attended in a very lovely bit of the Cadenberge Forest, and luckily it was a really beautiful sunny morning. He took as his text Romans, chapter 8, verse 37, and the Colonel read the lesson, St. Mark, chapter 12, verses 28 to 34. Hymns sung were "All people that on earth do dwell," "Praise, my soul, the King of Heaven," "O God, our help in ages past" and "Jerusalem," a most impressive service.

The next day, a member of the Regiment reported the fact that Willie Burki had been seen in Nijmegen, and so a jeep was sent for him at once. He had been liberated by the Canadians in the north of Holland, and altogether had survived the ordeal of a P.O.W. life extremely well. The Regiment was delighted to see him again.

At the same time Bob Hoare came back from leave, and took over as second-in-command, as Bernard was still away, and Peter Winslow continued to command 130 Battery.

CHAPTER EIGHT

Events after the Surrender

Narrative by Lieut.-Colonel J. S. Atkins, D.S.O., T.D., R.A.
ON 26th May the G.O.C. held a conference at Div. H.Q., situated west of Verden to tell us the future of the Division. Here I learned that the Division would be dismounted, and would take up its usual historic role of infantry once again. Likewise the artillery would be mostly dismounted, but that the Leicestershire Yeomanry had been warned that most of its younger members would probably have to go to S.E.A.C. in an S.P. role.

On 29th May many of us went to Delmanhorst to listen to a talk by the Corps Commander, General Horrocks. What a splendid man he is—loved and admired by everyone in the Corps. He gave us a most interesting and detailed account of the last part of the campaign—from the Reichswald Forest—crossing the Rhine—up to the final surrender. For two hours he kept us at a pitch of intense interest, with countless interesting stories. A really great man, what a splendid member of the House of Commons he would make. It was good to hear him pay such a high tribute to the Royal Regiment. "The biggest battle-winning factor of the whole Army" were his words.

Meanwhile, all ranks had been busily preparing for the visit to the Regiment by the G.O.C. on 1st June. A sad visit inasmuch as it was to be the last Regimental Parade of the Leicestershire Yeomanry in the Guards Armoured Division, after nearly four years training and campaigning with them.

All I can say is that, as Commanding Officer, I could not be prouder of my Regiment, and I think I cannot do better than to quote an account as written by an officer from Div. H.Q.

"A sight that would have gladdened the hearts of Leicestershire folk everywhere, was the farewell parade of 153rd Leicestershire Yeomanry Field Regiment, R.A., in a field near Bremen on 1st June.

"The Regiment, which has served the famous Guards Armoured Division throughout the Western Front campaign, was saying good-bye to the Guards, and the parade they staged for Major-General Allan Adair, C.B., D.S.O., M.C., commander of the Guards Division, was most impressive, even by Guards' standards.

"Self-propelled field-guns, observation-post tanks, scout cars and carriers, all spotless and gleaming in brilliant sunshine, were drawn up in review order, with their crews grouped alongside.

"Contrasting with the battleship grey guns and tanks, the shining green lorries of the Regiment were drawn up to right and left of the saluting base with echelon personnel, faultlessly turned out, lined up in front. It was an hour few, if any, of those present are ever likely to forget."

After inspecting the Regiment, General Adair mounted a rostrum, over which the Union Jack and the Leicestershire Yeomanry flags were flying. On the order "Break ranks, quick march," officers and men surrounded the rostrum and the General spoke.

He began by turning back the leaves of the chapter in the history that had just closed, a chapter the Regiment had helped to make great and glorious. He recalled the long, arduous series of exercises in various parts of England in which the gunners and the Guards had together learned the exacting technique of armoured warfare. He reminded them of the historic British advance of last September from Normandy to Brussels and on the approaches to Arnhem, every mile of it led by the Guards Armoured Division. The gunners had played their part in the gigantic barrages that opened two great battles of 1945, the Reichswald Forest battle, and the Rhine crossings battle.

Over the Rhine, the Guards had met the only tough opposition the German Army had put up in the west since the crossing of it, and had fought on to a fighting finish in the peninsular between Bremen and Hamburg.

"You all know it's been good," the General said, "on behalf of all the officers of the Brigade of Guards in this Division, I thank you for the wonderful support you have always given our armoured and infantry battalions. You know the secret of the finest teamwork. If there are new battles ahead for you I know you will never let down the very high standards you have always set yourselves. Wherever you may be in the future, I wish you all the very best of luck."

As commanding officer, I then replied to what the General had said, and spoke of the unfailing kindness and perfect co-operation the Regiment had always been given in the Division. "I know," I said, "that whenever the Leicestershire Yeomanry have a reunion dinner, we shall all agree, whatever may have happened to some of us in between, that the proudest days and moments of our service were those we spent with the Guards Armoured Division."

On Sunday, 3rd June, we held a Second Army Thanksgiving Service, being conducted by our padre, the Rev. W. March.

On 4th June Bob Hoare and I were invited to a party given by the officers of 1st Bn. Grenadier Guards, which proved to be a great success. I had a hazy recollection of an American band, magnificent fireworks, mainly produced by German flares and Very lights, the parade of the boats, which looked most effective mounted on jeeps, and driving through a waving cornfield, and last but not least, the General's fiery challenge of "Forty Years On" in reply to the "Eton Boating Song"—a great night.

On 6th June 130 Battery gave another of their, by now, famous concert parties, which will be remembered by many for its amusing Cockney turns, Lance-Bombadier Mitchell's playing, "A little bit of Frat," and the Battery choir under Sam Hughes. A very fitting anniversary to D-Day.

On 9th June one hundred officers and other ranks, and eight S.P.s represented the Regiment at the "Farewell-to-Armour Parade," to which the Commander-in-Chief and many other high-ranking generals came, mostly by air. The parade took place at Rotenburg aerodrome, and will be remembered for many a long day by those present. A full account by Major Hennessy is attached.

On 11th June Brigadier Norman came to speak to the Regiment to thank us for all our good work and say farewell to us, as we were about to leave the Division.

Shortly afterwards we learnt that we were not to leave the Division at present—this was a big mistake made by H.Q., R.A., alas, not the only one during the campaign.

This meant we looked rather stupid, having had our farewell parades, quite apart from the fact that we had done no reconnaissance in the Aachen area, to which the Division was going, some 300 miles away, and it also meant that no arrangements had been made to hand in our trucks, and we had to make the route in tanks and S.P.s, which had already gone much further than anticipated. We started on 18th June at 0600 hours from Achim and had a very interesting drive just skirting Hanover and west down the autobahn through part of the Ruhr to Cologne, all of which was flat, on through Duren and finally arrived at Geleen in Holland.

For some extraordinary reason only two S.P.s and ten tanks failed to make the grade, and they will soon be recovered from Hanover. It was a long, tiring and very hot journey for the drivers and crews of the S.P.s, but all came in smiling, knowing that they were out of the non-fraternisation country—at any rate for a while.

CHAPTER NINE

Farewell to Armour

TWO A.M. on a sultry June night in the year 1941—and the animated conversation which had started after the port was still in full swing.

"In the last war the Divisional sign was 'the ever-open eye,' wasn't it?"

"Will we get Covenanters or Valentines?"

"I doubt if I could tell the difference."

"Guardsmen weren't built for tanks anyway—they won't fit."

That evening we had heard that a Guards Division was to be formed and, what is more, an armoured division.

This chapter in the history of the Brigade of Guards, which for most of us began that night, has taken four years to write—a chapter of hard work, hard fighting and great triumphs. We have learnt the difference between a Covenanter and a Crusader—a Sherman and a Cromwell. And we have learned too that Guardsmen are built of the sort of material which will fit and stand up to any task that is given them.

And yesterday, on an airfield in the heart of defeated Germany, this glorious chapter was brought to a close—a fitting close—by the memorable words of Field-Marshal Montgomery.

Speaking of both the Guards Armoured Division and 6th Guards Armoured Brigade, he said: "I want to say, here and now, that in the sphere of armoured warfare the Guards have set a standard that it will be difficult for those who come after to reach . . . . . You will long be remembered for your prowess in armoured war. And now you are to return to your traditional role of infantry. We need you in the infantry! We need your high standards, your great efficiency in all matters, and your old traditions of duty and service...... and so I welcome you back into the infantry. You can look back with pride on your excursions into the realms of armoured warfare..."

On that June night in 1941 we had viewed our excursions into the realms of armoured warfare with the natural misgivings of the "new boy." We knew nothing of armoured warfare, but some of us, members of 7th Armoured Brigade—destined to become 5th Guards Armoured Brigade—knew a great deal about General Montgomery—destined to be Sir Bernard Montgomery—for, as Divisional Commander, he had skilfully withdrawn us to the beaches of Dunkirk. We knew him, above all, to be a man who meant what he said, and most of all we knew that in the realms of armoured warfare the traditions of the Brigade of Guards would be very much at stake. It is to those traditions that the credit must now fall. No one who, at that time was interested in the Guards Armoured Division, could have wished for them a higher tribute at the close of their task, and from no one could that tribute have come more sincerely. It will stand in the future, not for boastful pride, but as another great tradition which the Brigade has built for itself.

"And now you are to return to your traditional role of infantry." This came as no surprise as it had long been realised that, as soon as the job in Europe was done, this step was likely to be taken.

To some the tank may have been just a noisy, smelly, soulless conglomeration of metal, but to the vast majority of those who have nursed them, lived with them and fought with them, their relationship has taken on an almost human aspect. Sensitive to this, the Divisional Commander had decided that a great parade should take place to commemorate both the historic and the sentimental aspects of the event. "Farewell to Armour" he christened it after the Commander-in-Chief had kindly consented to take the Salute.

Rotenburg airfield was the side chosen—suitable for many reasons, including the fact that the town lay on the original axis of the Division, and had been captured in the operation which led to the crossing of the nearby autobahn, so cutting the enemy's communications between Hamburg and Bremen. For some days previously the Divisional Sappers had been busy setting the stage—but not so busy as results would lead one to believe. For though the saluting base grew overnight into an immaculate "Members' Enclosure", offset with glittering white ropes and flagpoles, and the bomb-scarred hayfield into a neatly cut green sward, the manual labour had been executed by a party of German prisoners who found themselves scraping ashes of the many Luftwaffe skeletons which littered the airfield and filling in the bomb craters made by the Air Forces which had done so much to bring them to their knees.

The parade was due to start at 1130 hours, and by 1045 hours the little airstrip which had been cut on the far end of the damaged airfield began to resemble Northolt during the Battle of Britain. At one time, fourteen Austers bearing fourteen red-tabbed sunrays were all circling round waiting to land. At that moment a large two-engined machine came in low over the trees. "Go away, you are too big for this strip" said a red rocket fired by the harassed flying-control officer. "Nonsense" (or words to that effect) said six red rockets which were immediately fired back at him, and in came General Gerry Feilden with a covey of sunrays from 21st Army Group. At 1115 hours, the Army Commander, General Dempsey, arrived, and then punctually at 1125 hours the Commander-in-Chief's plane circled over the parade ground and touched down—the thirty-eighth plane to grace the airstrip.

The Division was formed up on parade with the infantry battalions and representative detachments from the Services flanking the saluting base, while, stretched away to form an inverted "V," the armour and those gunner and signal units who were leaving the Division were formed up in three ranks—1200 infantry and some 250 tanks make an impressive sight.

In the centre of the arena were the massed bands of the Scots and Welsh Guards. In the enclosures were many thousands of spectators, not only members of neighbouring divisions but also airmen, sailors, Russians and even German prisoners who had come to admire their handiwork. In the sky the sun looked down on a truly splendid sight.

The Division had ended the war at Cuxhaven, and there, was found a large supply of naval paint. Shiny battleship grey, white hatches, black knobs, red tow-ropes and gaily striped aerials. "Peace has fair come on us with a vengeance" said a paint-smeared guardsman as we were driving round for a last look on the previous night. In short, the parade was not only present but very correct.

As the Commander-in-Chief drove up, escorted by a troop of 2nd Household Cavalry Regiment, and appeared on the saluting base, the Divisional Commander, standing centrally in the arena, called the Guards Armoured Division to attention for the General Salute.

After greeting the Field-Marshal, the inspection started, the party moving off in four half-tracks escorted by four armoured cars. In the leading vehicle travelled the Commander-in-Chief, the Divisional Commander and the Major-General, who had flown out from England on the previous night. In the second the Army Commander and the Commanders of 1st and 30th Corps, and in the third and fourth, a distinguished gathering from all three Services.

The inspection completed, the massed bands moved to a flank as the party once more took up its position on the dais for "the salute of the armour."

"Crews mount" from the Commander, 5th Guards Armoured Brigade—for two brief minutes the tanks looked like 250 bee-hives.

"Start up"—the air was rent by a great roar of engines. As each tank commander was ready he held his hand up. To the amazement and unbounded relief of the stage-managers, up went 250 hands.

And then, slowly and with great dignity, four columns from the four armoured battalions came out from the flanks and counter-marched across the parade-ground, turning to drive back over the hill. As each commander passed the Field-Marshal he traversed his gun and himself saluted. As the last files crossed each other the central block at the back of the triangle drew away, the diesel engines of the self-propelled anti-tank guns leaving their usual pall of blue smoke, which added greatly to the effect.

As their turrets slowly disappeared over the horizon and the roar of engines changed to a distant rumble, the massed bands took up the strains of Auld Lang Syne until the last chorus faded out to complete silence.

* * * *

"What," one can hear the cynic saying, "can possibly be moving about seeing a lot of battered old monsters of destruction disappearing over a hill ? "

The answer is, "Nothing, unless you saw them do it."

Many of those old friends had landed over the Normandy beaches almost exactly a year ago and had come up through France, Belgium, Holland and half Germany on their tracks. We were grateful that none had failed us even for this last supreme effort.

The infantry, who had stood respectfully at attention during the salute, now turned inwards towards the dais and stood at ease while the massed bands wheeled into the centre of the arena and marched away up the hill towards the crest, where 2nd Household Cavalry Regiment, now the Divisional reconnaissance regiment, alone had remained in position. As they approached, the heads and shoulders of marching infantry began to appear over the horizon. A pause on the line of the armoured cars and then the command "Brigades, by the centre, quick march." Five columns of "armoured infantry" from 2nd Grenadier Guards, 2nd Irish Guards, 2nd Welsh Guards and 1st Coldstream Guards, with a composite column from 6th Guards Brigade in the centre, swung down the centre of the arena while the massed bands played each regimental march in turn.

Can it be that the cramped living conditions of a tank crew prompt them to stretch and exert their limbs the more vigorously when let loose ? At all events, these former tank men came forward to take up their position as infantry in the ranks of the newly formed division in such style that not even the deep ruts, cut a few minutes earlier by their own tanks as a last protest to their banishment, could throw them out. The Coldstream column on the left flank ran into early opposition from a dachshund who fought a typically senseless and fanatical rearguard action over the last 200 yards, and then, realising that his encirclement was complete, resorted to unnatural intercourse with a *schnautzer* as a sulky gesture of defiance during the playing of "The King."

The scene now presented eleven columns of infantry in sixes facing the saluting base. Behind them the massed bands of the Scots and Welsh Guards, and, in rear, strung out in a single line, a squadron of 2nd Household Cavalry Regiment.

For the first time the Divisional Commander called the Guards Division to attention. "God Save the King"—and the ceremony was over.

"The Division is dead—long live the Division."

Field-Marshal Montgomery then called on the assembled company to gather round, and delivered the address which is repeated here below.

The Field-Marshal began by saying that the German war being over, it was interesting to consider how it was that we had won when in 1940 and 1941 and even in 1942 it had seemed quite impossible that we should ever win. There were many reasons for this, but he always considered that there were two reasons which were basically the main cause of the enemy's defeat.

Firstly, the great mistakes made by the enemy, beginning in 1941 when the Germans attacked Russia and Japan attacked the Americans, thus bringing these two great nations in on our side.

Secondly, the good fighting qualities of the Allied soldiers among whom the fighting man of the British Empire stands out in a proud position.

The Field-Marshal then went on to speak as follows:—

"And now I want to say something about your Division.

"When this war began the Guards were infantry.

"At a time of great national danger in 1941 the Guards formed armoured formations. The Guards Armoured Division and the 6th Guards Armoured Brigade fought throughout this historic campaign in Western Europe.

"I don't suppose there is any officer in the Army who can speak with such weight of experience as myself about the relative standards of battle efficiency of this or that formation or unit. From Alamein to the Baltic, I have had many formations and units under my command.

"I want to say, here and now, that in the sphere of armoured warfare the Guards have set a standard that it will be difficult for those that come after to reach.

"In modern war it is the co-operation of all arms, armoured and un-armoured, that wins the battle, and in this respect you have achieved great results. In fact, the Guards have shown that whatever they are asked to do—whatever they take on—they do well; maintaining always the highest standards and giving a lead to all others. You will long be remembered for your prowess in armoured war. And now you are to return to your traditional role of infantry.

"Some of you may wonder why this is so. There are many reasons. First: the King wishes it. Second: the Brigade of Guards as a whole are anxious that this should be done.

"And third: I myself, an infantry soldier of many years' service would say to you that you are needed in the infantry. The infantry arm has come right to the fore in this war; it is the most versatile of all arms; nothing can be done without infantry to help; there is never enough infantry for the tasks that have to be done.

"It is vital that the infantry of the British Army should be a firm and strong rock on which to build the post-war Army; it is the central core of the fighting machine, on which all else depends.

"We need you in the infantry; we need your high standards; your great efficiency in all matters, and your old traditions of duty and service; all these are needed to help weld the infantry arm into a firm and solid basis on which to build.

"And so I welcome you back into the infantry.

"You can look back with pride on your excursion into the realms of armoured warfare; and the experience there gained will always be valuable to you"

The Field-Marshal finally made the following remarks about the divisional commander.

"I don't know whether the officers and men of the Guards Armoured Division realise how much they owe to General Allan Adair. From my position as Commander-in-Chief I know the answer to this straight away, and I can tell you that answer.

"General Allan trained the Division in England; he then took it across the channel to Normandy and commanded it there in the great battles of the Seine; he then led it through France; through Belgium, through Holland, then into Germany, and commanded it till the war ended.

"Throughout all this time he never failed me and he never failed you; he gave of his best, that the Division might do well in battle, and he has reaped his full reward. You owe more to him than you can ever repay. And I will go further, I would say that the Brigade of Guards was lucky to have an officer like General Allan to handle this armoured matter for them, few officers could have done it so well. In front of you all I wish to congratulate General Allan on having brought the matter to such a successful conclusion."

The obvious sincerity of this truly generous tribute was tremendously appreciated by the members of the Division, who felt doubly grateful to the Commander-in-Chief for expressing in his own words the views we have so long held about our Divisional-Commander.

The ceremony was over, but the day was not. It is in the best Continental tradition that a funeral should provide an excuse for the most monumental gastronomic excesses. The administrative staffs of Divisional and Brigade Headquarters had consequently put their heads, their guile and their most experienced fraternisers together and produced in a neighbouring field a scene akin to the Field of the Cloth of Gold.

Once again the versatile German prisoners had been pressed into service. From a flagstaff in the centre of the grass enclosure fluttered the Brigade flag. The bands played, and in the flower-bedecked luncheon tents salvo after salvo of corks acclaimed the Order of the Day, whilst those responsible for producing asparagus and strawberries and cream had shown a proper appreciation of the circumstances. After all, our war was over—and looking round here were most of the members of the winning team. Perhaps not since it started has the "first eleven" found themselves in such a position to let their hair down from beneath the fetters of their red hats. And besides, it was Derby Day.

In the far corner was the familiar number board with the runners. And there the equally familiar queues in and out of the tote tent. "All I need to see now is a man in a top-hat and frock-coat hacking down to the starting gate and I shall know once and for all that champagne on a hot day can prove treacherous," I said to myself.

But there sure enough was the starter himself, getting up on his little grey cob and trotting off across the fields, his top hat glistening in the afternoon sun.

From a loudspeaker poised in the trees over our heads Raymond Glendenning was describing the scene on Newmarket Heath.

"There they go, cantering down to the start," he said, and there before our eyes were eight "requisitioned" mounts ridden in the best professional style by gaily adorned jockeys to an improvised starting gate erected on the far side of the field.

The scene at the starting gate was slightly less animated than the one now being described by Frank O'Farrell, but after a certain amount of pressure they all got away and were last seen heading in the direction of Rotenburg main street, where the "starter" had a date with the local undertaker who was anxiously awaiting the return of his top-hat and frock-coat for tomorrow's ceremony. Their fade-out was less impressive, though far more sensational, than that provided by the Shermans earlier in the day.

Over to the grandstand—Dante coming through on the rails—the favourite wins—a fitting end to a great day.

Staggered over the next two hours, the "greater red-tabbed sunrays" staggered their respective ways to the car-park or the air-strip until finally the twin-engined monster from the 21st Army Group drew up for its perilous take-off. So light were the heads of the passengers, however, that the party became airborne almost immediately, firing a salvo of red rockets in a *feu de joie* as they went.

* * * *

On 28th July 1945 contingents representing Regiments in the Guards Armoured Division, who had relieved Brussels in 1944, paraded outside the Palais de Justice.

During a most impressive ceremony, the Commanding Officer, Lt.-Colonel J. S. Atkins, D.S.O., T.D., was presented with a plaque by Monsieur M. J. Van der Meulehoeck, Burgomaster of Brussels. The inscription on this read as follows: "Presented by the people of Brussels to the 153rd (Leicestershire Yeomanry) Field Regt. R.A., in gratitude for the part they played in the Guards Armoured Division's liberation of Brussels, Sept. 3rd., 1944."

Of the official party there were present, H.M. Queen Elizabeth of the Belgians, M. J. Van Meulebroeck, Burgomaster of Brussels, Carl Van Roey, Archbishop of Malines, Prince Jean of Luxembourg, Sir Hugh and Lady Knatchbull-Hugessen, K.C.M.G., British Ambassador, Lt.-General Sir Charles Lloyd, K.C.B., C.B., D.S.O., M.C., Brigade of Guards.

CHAPTER TEN

In Conclusion

THERE are two things which if left out would make this history incomplete. Firstly, the fact that Lt.-Colonel Jock Atkins returned to civilian life on the 18th August 1945. It was largely due to his enthusiasm in the many months of training before arriving in France that the Regiment was in such splendid spirits and so confident in itself when it landed. It was in no less measure due to his splendid leadership throughout the battles, that the Regiment acquitted itself so well in the campaign. His going was felt deeply by all ranks.

Secondly, a brief note on the role the Regiment was called upon to play in the Army of Occupation. When the Division moved to its allotted area for occupational duties, based on Bad Godesberg and Cologne, the Regiment was under the impression that it was going to S.E.A.C., and was to stay put for the time being in the Bremen area. However, at the last minute these orders were cancelled, and it moved with the Division. All the area had already been sub-allotted, and as it was found that there was no room left, it was therefore ordered to Geleen in Holland, close to the Dutch-German border, and a part well known to all who were there in November, 1944, when R.H.Q. was quite close at Hillensberg.

For quite a long time it was still thought that the Regiment was going to S.E.A.C., and so it kept its full complement of guns and tanks. Eventually it was heard that this was not so, and they were finally taken away to Antwerp on the 15th October. To many it was a sad sight to see them lumbering off on their transporters. They had served the Regiment so well, and played a big part in the eventual and complete defeat of Hitler's master race.

During this period General Allan Adair came to pay the Regiment a farewell visit, as he was shortly due to return to England. He arrived in an Air O.P. with his A.D.C., Aylmer Tryon, on the Beek Airstrip on the 12th September, 1945. He was most impressed with Roy Clark's Educational Centre, which he had built out of the ruins of some bungalows. After walking round the Regiment and talking to a number of the men, he and the C.R.A., Brigadier Ebbles, C.B.E., M.C., lunched at R.H.Q.

At the beginning of October orders were received that the Regiment would move into Brand Barracks, on the outskirts of Aachen. The town itself had been captured by the Americans when the Siegfried Line was first penetrated, and it had also had short but sharp visits from the British and American Air Forces, with the result that it did not look the happiest of cities.

However, the barracks which were shared with the 75th Anti-Tank Regiment, R.A., were not greatly damaged. The main trouble was that they had been housing twelve thousand Russian displaced personnel, and it was a major problem to have every room satisfactorily de-loused. However, this was eventually accomplished successfully by the hygiene authorities, and the R.E.s made a very good job of the re-decorating.

As soon as the Regiment was settled in its new quarters, it started to take up its occupational role. This entailed many tasks, the main one being the control of the Geilenkirchen Landkreis. This was a large area, with about twenty-eight miles of frontier, and eighty-five square miles in all, an area which had been very heavily fought over by the British and the Americans. It contained some of the best sited and most strongly defended bits of the Siegfried Line, and when such defences are seen, there can be little doubt left in anyone's mind that the German Staff knew their job, and knew it well.

Another of the tasks was to clear the area of all armaments. A vast amount of every type of ammunition, British, American and German, a lot of it in a highly dangerous state, lies all over the area, and it is a lengthy and tedious performance having it removed with German labour!

There are also three coal-mines which have to be taken care of in case the civilian population attempt to help themselves, not to mention curfew patrols, and a frontier post to be manned. Over and above all this there are various guard duties to be carried out in Aachen, so it is rarely that the Battery Commanders see much of their men.

To all appearances, the Regiment will be broken up probably in the summer of 1946. No Yeoman will be left by then, either officers or other ranks, and perhaps it will be all for the best. For by then, the present-day Government should have decided on the future of the Territorial Army, in which the Leicestershire Yeomanry will be ready to take up its rightful place once more.

Brand Barracks,
Aachen,
Germany,
December, 1945.

www.ingramcontent.com/pod-product-compliance
Lightning Source LLC
Chambersburg PA
CBHW072048160426
43197CB00014B/2679